T0047255

MONTMARTRE

ALSO BY JOHN BAXTER

Saint-Germain-des-Prés

Five Nights in Paris

Paris at the End of the World

The Perfect Meal

The Most Beautiful Walk in the World

Von Sternberg

Carnal Knowledge

Immoveable Feast

We'll Always Have Paris

A Pound of Paper

Science Fiction in the Cinema

Buñuel

Fellini

Stanley Kubrick

Steven Spielberg

Woody Allen

George Lucas

De Niro

TRANSLATED BY JOHN BAXTER

My Lady Opium by Claude Farrère

Morphine by Jean-Louis Dubut de Laforest

The Diary of a Chambermaid by Octave Mirbeau

Gamiani, or Two Nights of Excess by Alfred de Musset

MONTMARTRE

*Paris's Village of
Art and Sin*

John Baxter

HARPER ● PERENNIAL

NEW YORK ● LONDON ● TORONTO ● SYDNEY ● NEW DELHI ● AUCKLAND

MONTMARTRE. Copyright © 2017 by John Baxter. All rights reserved. Printed in the United States of America. No part of this book may be used or reproduced in any manner whatsoever without written permission except in the case of brief quotations embodied in critical articles and reviews. For information, address HarperCollins Publishers, 195 Broadway, New York, NY 10007.

HarperCollins books may be purchased for educational, business, or sales promotional use. For information, please email the Special Markets Department at SPsales@harper collins.com.

FIRST EDITION

Map by Tony Foster

Library of Congress Cataloging-in-Publication Data has been applied for.

ISBN 978-0-06-243189-9

17 18 19 20 21   LSC   10 9 8 7 6 5 4 3 2 1

For Marie-Dominique,
without whom . . .

Entrance to Cabaret of Hell, 1899. (Edouard Cucuel)

Contents

VIII

Contents

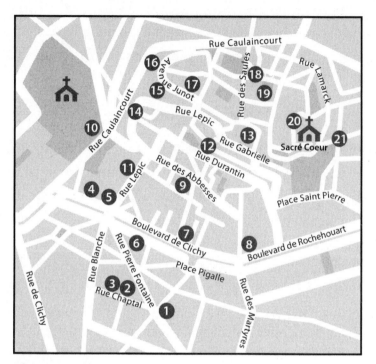

Montmartre

MONTMARTRE

ON THE FIRST WARM DAY IN MAY . . .

THERE ARE CERTAIN MORNINGS IN EARLY SPRING WHEN women, on a whim, decide it's the day to start going bare-legged or to wear a hat, while men loop a scarf around their neck and shake the creases out of the linen jacket stuffed in the back of the closet since September.

Jane came from somewhere in the Midwest. Each spring, France fills with women like her. They appear overnight, just as drifting dandelion seeds cover Europe in thistledown. Like those seeds, they follow wind and whim from London to Rome to Berlin to Paris, looking for something that Des Moines, Iowa, or Rapid City, South Dakota, doesn't provide—girls of summer who, as Stephen Sondheim explains in his song of that name, may, in contracting "a touch of the sun," also incur "a touch of the moon."

In Paris, these lost ladies take a cooking course at Le Cordon Bleu, a refresher class in conversational French at the Alliance Française, attend readings at Shakespeare and Company or the American Library, even risk a flirtation with someone met in a café. But if they are readers, they sign up for walking tours around the haunts of Hemingway, Fitzgerald, Gertrude Stein, and other expatriate writers.

This is where I meet them, since, for Anglophones who have made their lives here, the role of guide, interpreter, and "someone I know in Paris" comes with the territory.

I'd agreed to show Jane and her traveling companion around the literary sites of Saint-Germain-des-Prés, but when we met that Sunday morning, she was alone.

"My friend didn't feel up to it," she explained. "He decided to stay at the hotel."

I could visualize the type; a little hungover, a little lazy, and not all that interested in writers he hoped he'd left behind in American Literature 101.

"That's a pity," I said, glancing at the cloudless sky. "The weather's perfect."

She looked wistful. "We'd booked a tour of Montmartre yesterday," she said, "but he said he couldn't face all those hills, so we didn't do that, either. I'm really sorry to have missed it."

"Well," I said, "would you rather go to Montmartre today instead of Saint-Germain?"

"Oh, that's not necessary," she said, surprised.

"It's no problem," I said. "Saint-Germain has waited five centuries. It'll still be here when you want to see it."

So we took the bus up Boulevard Saint-Michel, and thirty minutes later, the funicular car carried us the last few hundred meters to the summit of Montmartre, the steep-sided 170-meter-high tableland on the northern edge of the city that Parisians call *la butte.*

The bulbous white domes of the Basilica of Sacré-Coeur loomed above us, reminding me, as usual, of a cluster of mushrooms. "Grandiose rather than beautiful," thought one architectural historian, trying to be kind.

Hundreds of visitors were already sitting on the steps below the cathedral or leaning on the balustrade of the terrace that, like a box at the opera, offers an unrivaled panorama of the city. Some were simply enjoying the morning, others listening to Paraguayan harpist Hugo Barahona, as much a fixture of Montmartre as the caricaturists on Place du Tertre vying to draw your portrait.

He'd claimed his usual spot, on the steps below the promenade, facing away from the city—a shrewd choice,

The Basilica of Sacré-Coeur.

since the whole of Paris provided him with an unsurpassable backdrop. He agreed with Gertrude Stein's companion, Alice Toklas, who said, "I like a good view, but I prefer to sit with my back to it."

His harp's metallic zither-like jangle, hinting at a tonal tradition remote from here, was one more element among the thousands that made up Montmartre's unique personality. Here, even music has a touch of strange. As he paused between numbers, I dropped five euros into his basket and murmured a request.

In better weather, a few mute "living statues," skin painted chalk-white, pose at the foot of the stairs leading up the church. One, standing on a plinth, his knees at our face level, wore the robe and laurel wreath of an Italian Renaissance scholar. Had he chosen to speak, the man might have explained that his outfit copied that worn by Dante as fellow poet Virgil led him on a tour of Hell in *The Divine Comedy*. Any such explanation, however, would have been a waste of time, since not many American colleges teach early Italian poetry (or poetry of any kind), and few visitors catch the reference.

I photographed the two together, the modern Dante unbending sufficiently to lift a marmoreal hand above Jane's head in benediction. At that instant, Barahona began playing the tune I'd requested, "La Complainte de la Butte" ("The Lament of the Butte")—the theme for the Jean Renoir film *French Cancan*. Georges van Parys's melancholy waltz filtered through the tourist chatter, carrying its message of loneliness and isolation.

The stairways up to *la butte* can make the wretched
    sigh,
While windmill wings of the *moulins* shelter you
    and I . . .

Time to go, before the perfect moment passed.

"What a marvelous day," Jane said later, over lunch on
the terrace of our apartment. "I'm so glad we went."

"I'm sorry your friend couldn't be with us."

She turned her head away and looked out over the
roofs of Paris, as if she couldn't quite remember who I was
talking about.

"We haven't been together for long," she said at last,
"and we've never done a trip like this. I hoped . . ."

She paused, then said with a sense of a mind made up,
"I'm going to leave him."

I laughed.

"What's so funny?" she asked, a little annoyed.

"Oh, nothing."

But I could only think, *Chalk up another victory for
Montmartre.*

INTRODUCTION

We all know places in the world where consciousness slows, and the soul, however briefly, achieves repose. For me, one of them is a bridge over the shallow stream that runs through the home of the impressionist painter Claude Monet at Giverny. Watching water plants entwine in the slowly flowing water induces the same calm I felt in Japan while contemplating a few square meters of gravel and some ancient stones in the imperial gardens of Kyoto. Though on opposite sides of the world, each evoked the same timeless tranquility.

Other locations excite rather than relax us. Like those that encourage reflection, they are no respecter of antiquity: sparks struck from old stones burn as fiercely as those from the new. But where those sparks fall, passions ignite, sometimes illuminating, at other times destroying.

Again, the effect is subjective. No matter how deeply I breathe the air of Berlin, I have yet to detect even a whiff of the legendary *Berliner Luft* or Berlin Air, an invisible gas that supposedly rises from marshes beneath that city, in-

The water lily garden at Claude Monet's Giverny home.

spiring and exciting. If I felt that exhilaration anywhere, it was in Los Angeles, where I often woke to a sense of infinite possibility, and ready, as Lewis Carroll wrote, to "believe as many as six impossible things before breakfast."

In Paris, one district more than any other demonstrates this capacity to induce in people a readiness, even a hunger, for change. Though superficially tranquil, Montmartre, the hilltop village on the city's northern edge, has repeatedly erupted in revolution—in art, in politics, in culture—and left the world fundamentally changed.

Given its sleepy beginnings, who could have foreseen that, within a few years of becoming part of the city in 1860, events in Montmartre would grip the world?

As a Prussian army ringed Paris, starving it of munitions, food, even water, the wind that had only ever driven flour mills was harnessed to carry news-laden balloons above enemy lines.

Barely was the siege lifted than Montmartre declared itself an anarchist state, the Commune, independent of both Paris and the nation. Yet, within a generation, it turned its back on politics to become a laboratory of experiment in painting—only to discard art also, and re-emerge as a community synonymous with sensuality and sex. Of all these upheavals, however, only ruins, statues, and memorials remain. It's as if each sweep of history expunges what went before, as an eraser wipes a blackboard clean.

Today Montmartre is quiet once again. But only someone with no sense of history would gamble on it remaining so. Repeatedly its citizens have demonstrated a capacity for self-transformation. They set the world on fire more than once in the past. They may yet do so again.

But what else would you expect of a nation with a patron saint like Denis?

1

LOSING YOUR HEAD

THE LONG WALK OF SAINT DENIS

Among the statues flanking the main entrance to the cathedral of Notre Dame is one of a man cradling his own severed head. He is Saint Denis (pronounced Der-*ny*), who, if legend is to believed, walked for kilometers in this state while his head never stopped preaching.

Even more than most tales from the third century, stories about Denis need to be taken on faith. Most can only be traced back to AD 500 and a life of Saint Genevieve written by one of her followers. It was Genevieve, through this scribe, who described how, around AD 250, when Lutèce or Lutetia, as Paris was then known, was still an outpost of Rome, a Denys or maybe Dionysius and six other priests arrived in the valley of the Seine. Sent by Pope Fabian, they had orders to convert the heathen Gauls. Fabian having since died, however, the seven were on their own.

Their arrival troubled the local prefect, Sisinnius Fesceninus. No colonial administrator ever forgot what had happened in Judaea two centuries earlier when a charismatic zealot, with only a handful of followers, plunged the region into chaos, interrupting trade and committing the army to an expensive police action. Pontius Pilate, the prefect who tried to wash his hands of the whole business, leaving it to be settled by the locals, not only lost his job but committed suicide.

After that, Rome cracked down on Christianity. To remind citizens where their loyalty lay, the law required every Roman to sacrifice to the gods at least once each year, and produce a certificate to prove they'd done so.

Summoning Denis and his two lieutenants, Rusticus and Eleutherius, the prefect suggested they slaughter an animal or offer some other tribute to one of Rome's numerous deities. The trio refused. Even more provocatively, Denis installed himself on the Île de la Cité, near the present site of Notre Dame, appointed himself and his two followers bishops, and urged local Christians not only to ignore the law on sacrifice but to attack the temples where Romans worshipped.

What followed can scarcely have been a surprise to either Denis or his acolytes. Brought before Sisinnius for the second time, they were elaborately tortured, but still refused to submit. Seeing little alternative, the prefect ordered them publicly beheaded. At the same time, he launched a general purge of Christians. In case the lesson should be lost on the locals, the decapitations were to take place before the temple of the god Mercury, on the summit of the highest point around, a nameless bluff to the north, soon to become known as the hill of the martyr: Montmartre.

But soldiers being soldiers, the men detailed to execute Denis and his acolytes took one look at the steep hillside and decided to kill them lower down the slope, and toss their bodies into the Seine, then, as now, a convenient way to dispose of embarrassing evidence.

The prospect of an execution drew spectators, including some of Denis's followers, among them a wealthy Roman lady, Catulla. Once she enters the story, however, accounts of the execution and its aftermath begin to diverge.

Officially, all three men were decapitated and their corpses thrown into the Seine, to be recovered by their followers and, under Catulla's direction, given decent burial. In the unofficial version, however, Denis, on losing his head, is said to have calmly picked it up from the mud and set off up the hill. Even more astonishing, as he walked, his head continued to speak, preaching a sermon on love and forgiveness. Trailed by Catulla and a wondering crowd, he carried it up the slope of Montmartre, pausing at a spring to wash the blood from his face. Still declaiming, he crossed the butte and ambled down the other side. Four miles farther on, at Catolacus, Catulla's estate, he handed her his head, lay down, and died. She buried him on the spot, from which wheat and other plants sprouted: proof, claimed Catulla and her fellow believers, of his divine status. Reflecting this aspect of the legend, images of Denis often show vines or flowers where his head should be.

Could there be a grain of truth lurking in this fantastic tale? A few details give it slight credibility. As buried seeds germinate on exposure to sunlight, flowers and greenery often grow on new graves. As for the severed head and the sermon, execution by sword was, literally, hit or miss. A clumsy swipe could strike the back of the head rather than the neck, slicing off part of the skull. Had this happened to Denis, he might have survived such an injury for a short time, even mumbled a few words; enough, anyway, for gossip to amplify into a sermon.

As Rome's influence waned in Gaul and Christianity spread through the Frankish kingdom that replaced it, so did the tale of Denis's headless promenade. Despite this, five hundred years passed before he was canonized. If progress was slow, blame it on the curious fact that he wasn't the only martyr reputed to have survived beheading. By one count, there were 134 of them—enough to have their own designation: cephalophores.

Saint Denis preaches to astonished Romans. (Joseph Kuhn-Régnier)

Before it recognizes a saint, the church requires evidence of miracles performed in his or her name. On this count, Denis was a winner. Because of his calm in the face of death, praying to him was credited with subduing the frenzy of someone bitten by a rabid animal, and even with driving out devils from those possessed by them. More prosaically, a quick appeal to Denis was said to cure a headache.

Why select Denis as France's patron saint and not someone more proactive, like the tireless Saint Genevieve? She's credited with organizing the "prayer marathon" in 451 that dissuaded that fifth-century Hitler, Attila the Hun, from sacking the city, for which she received the lesser role of patron of Paris alone. Was it because not even decapitation stopped Denis from talking? Who better, the church may have reasoned, to represent a nation for which conversation is almost as important as life itself?

WHERE DENIS DIED

Because of the church's endorsement, Denis didn't drift off into the limbo of the remaining 133 cephalophores but lingered in the limelight, not displaced even by such flamboyant rivals as Joan of Arc. Shrines were built at every stop on his miraculous stroll, some of them, as in the case of Sacré-Coeur, adapted to venerate more modern examples of sacrifice as well.

In the half millennium following his death, scholars with a knowledge of mythology noticed how much his story paralleled the myth of Orpheus, whose head, ripped off by his female admirers and thrown in the ocean, continued to sing while his hands accompanied him on the lyre. Of this theory, approaching heresy, the wisest said nothing; heretics tended to end up burned at the stake. Besides, there was wisdom in letting the unlettered cling to their dreams. As a twentieth-century savant succinctly put it, "When the legend becomes fact, print the legend."

Traditionally, the actual site of Denis's execution is now occupied by the Metro station of Abbesses, halfway up the southern slope of Montmartre. Quick to remind us of its past, Montmartre has matched stops on Denis's walk to reminders of contemporary tyranny. On rue Yvonne Le Tac, named for a World War II schoolmistress and survivor of both Birkenau and Auschwitz concentration camps, a discreet basement Martyrs' Chapel marks the spring where Denis paused to wash his face before continuing to the summit. The point at which he's assumed to have crossed the butte is in a park he shares with another resistance heroine, Suzanne Buisson. Here, Denis receives the added honor of a statue, although the sculptor skimped on research. The saint's miter, the tall headgear signifying a bishop, didn't become part of the official regalia until five hundred years after his death.

At Catolacus, where Catulla buried him, Saint Genevieve, around 475, erected a larger church. Over the next four centuries, Catolacus became the town of Saint-Denis and the church metamorphosed into a Gothic cathedral where France's queens were crowned, and the bodies of royalty laid to rest in its crypt. Inspired by the myth of grain and flowers growing on Denis's grave, Benedictine monks founded an abbey on the summit of Montmartre and planted orchards and vineyards.

If Denis hoped to rest in peace after his walk, he was disappointed. His bones and other saints, as well as former rulers of France, were interred in the crypt of the Saint-Denis cathedral. They remained there until 1789, when revolutionary mobs, believing everything in the church belonged to kings and queens, dragged out the skeletons of royalty and saints alike, and used their skulls for ball games. Some churches later claimed to have rescued a few fragments of the saint, notably his jawbone and the top of his skull, but if anything of Denis truly survives, it's the tale of his bizarre death and its aftermath, more durable than anything of the flesh. Were he here to advise us, one feels he would agree with the contemporary writer's advice: print the legend.

2

THE CAT THAT WALKED BY ITSELF

For Henri de Toulouse-Lautrec, Vincent van Gogh, and Pablo Picasso, life in Montmartre at the end of the nineteenth century was made more endurable by the outdoor bars called *buvettes* and *guinguettes* where they could argue art all night over a few bottles of wine. Occasionally someone sang or recited a poem, but the real business was talk, lubricated with the cheapest wine in the cellar.

From time to time, they glanced down the hill at the lights of Boulevard de Clichy. Perhaps they heard a snatch of music from the Abbaye de Thélème and Au Rat Mort, up-market cabarets that maintained private rooms upstairs for the use of the gaudier whores and their clients. One British writer, lubriciously disapproving, called the bars of Clichy and Pigalle "cosmopolitan haunts of facile pleasure where those fond of nocturnal rambles could wander from cabaret to cabaret till dawn."

The butte prided itself on preferring intellectual pleasure to the physical variety. The first to provide it professionally was Rodolphe Salis.

In 1881, Salis was a middle-aged artist scratching a precarious living carving figures for Stations of the Cross, the series of fourteen reliefs illustrating the agony and death of Christ that decorate the walls of every church as an aid to meditation. With few new churches being built, business was so bad that Salis's wife resorted to prostitution to keep food on the table.

Wandering Montmartre, a depressed Salis passed an empty two-room shop on Boulevard de Rochechouart, the busy avenue circling the butte. Inside, a black cat yowled, echoing his state of mind. It also gave him an idea. Reasoning that the friends with whom he'd shared so many nights in gloomy *buvettes* might enjoy one where the lights were brighter and the entertainment more stimulating, he rented the shop and opened a *café-concert* he called Le Chat Noir (The Black Cat). Yvette Guilbert, a star of the Moulin Rouge and a friend, confirmed the story. "An old black tomcat he found in that first tiny shop gave Salis the name," she said. "It became his mascot."

In choosing a black cat as his trademark, Salis defied tradition. Not only were they associated with witchcraft and bad luck; felines of all sorts were disliked by most Frenchmen, who preferred dogs. Cats had even sparked a rebellion in the 1730s among the apprentice printers of Paris. Resenting their employers feeding scraps to their pets while they went hungry, the apprentices kept up a nightly chorus of catlike yowling until the printers agreed that the cats should go. Hundreds were rounded up and massacred.

Salis persuaded some heavy-drinking friends from the Right Bank to transfer their custom to his place. Calling themselves the Hydrophobes or Water-Haters because of their preference for wine over water, they enjoyed the relative innocence of the butte, particularly since Salis served better wine, and also enlivened their evenings with witty monologues. As in twenties Berlin or Greenwich Village in the sixties, satiric humor found an appreciative audience. Salis relocated in a four-story house, formerly the home of painter Alfred Stevens, at 12 rue Victor Massé. Artist friends decorated the new premises with fake antiques, including part of an infant skeleton, labeled "The Skull of King Louis XIII as a Child." The doorman dressed, for no very good reason, in the uniform of the Swiss Guard, the elite unit charged with protecting the pope in the Vatican.

Le Chat Noir was the first cabaret to offer more than "facile pleasure." As one historian wrote, "It was the Chat Noir which first led the ordinary pleasure-seeker to appreciate the joys of *la butte*. There for a few francs the visitor fond of art and laughter was allowed to participate in the joys of Bohemian life, to hear clever and amusing songs sung by their authors while surrounded by a Rabelaisian atmosphere."

Convinced more than ever that the black cat had brought him luck, Salis asked Théophile Steinlen to create a hanging sign and a poster using its image. Steinlen's cat, staring imperiously at the world through golden eyes, became almost as familiar as Toulouse-Lautrec's posters for the Moulin Rouge, and launched Steinlen as the preeminent illustrator of Montmartre.

Le Chat Noir was soon the hottest venue in Montmartre, frequented, wrote one patron, by "a fantastic mixture of writers and painters, journalists and students, not to mention the *demi-mondaines* and respectable ladies looking for a lively scene." Further to demonstrate his independence, Salis installed a piano, frowned on by rivals as inconsistent with cabaret tradition and by the police as too noisy. Ignoring both, Salis hired composer Erik Satie as his pianist. A true eccentric, Satie lived in an apartment dominated by two grand pianos, one balanced on top of the other. Each day, he walked ten kilometers to the Chat Noir, invariably carrying an umbrella, wearing rimless glasses, a bowler hat, and dressed in the only thing he ever wore, one of seven identical gray suits bought after a financial windfall.

Poster for Chat Noir cabaret, 1896. (Théophile Steinlen)

Nothing in his manner suggested the composer of such delicate piano pieces as "Trois Morceaux en forme de Poire" ("Three Pieces in the Shape of a Pear") and the languid, melancholy waltzes "Gymnopédies" and "Gnossiennes," inspired by images of Cretan temple dancers.

As audiences swelled to over two hundred a night, Salis moved again, this time to 68 Boulevard de Clichy, close enough to the Moulin Rouge for some of its stars, including Jane Avril and Yvette Guilbert, to moonlight for him. Toulouse-Lautrec became a regular, while Satie's music attracted such fellow composers as Claude Debussy.

The show also went on tour, playing in halls all over France and turning Steinlen's black cat into a nationally recognized symbol of bohemian Paris. Salis died in 1896, but the cat outlived both the cabaret and its founder. "Rodolphe Salis had wrung the neck of the old medieval fear of the black cat," wrote one historian, "making it a symbol of imagination, intelligence and satirical humor." It was a rehabilitation long overdue.

Rue Maurice Utrillo.

THE CAT IN THE FLAT

A STORY OF MODERN MONTMARTRE

Clive, an American journalist friend, had just moved to France from Los Angeles. Searching for an apartment, he found, with the help of a small local agency, the very place he wanted. A compact studio in Montmartre, fully furnished, it perched halfway up rue Maurice Utrillo, not a street at all, but one of the stone staircases that climb the hill toward the Basilica of Sacré-Coeur.

The agent managed the property for the owner, who lived in Australia. Clive didn't inquire too closely; just signed a three-year lease, paid his deposit, and installed his few belongings, including his companion of many years, a sleek black cat named Brutus.

Never having met his landlord and only vaguely aware of his name, Clive was surprised, returning home one afternoon a few weeks later, to find a middle-aged man sitting on a suitcase outside his front door.

"Name's Bill Ellington," the man said genially in a heavy Australian accent, offering his hand. "This is my place."

Over coffee, Ellington explained he was on a last-minute business trip and hadn't booked a hotel room. Would Clive mind if he crashed on the couch for a night?

Well, it is *his place,* thought Clive, not terribly enthusiastic. Leaving Ellington to unpack, he walked down to the market to shop for dinner.

Returning an hour later, he found that his key no longer opened the front door. Peering at the lock, he saw a shiny new key plate. During his absence, someone had replaced it. With a growing sense of the unreal, he shaded his eyes and looked through the window. All he saw were the furnishings that had been there when he moved in. Of his possessions—photographs, kitchen utensils, even Brutus—there was no sign.

Prolonged pounding brought Ellington to the door.

"Yes?" said the Australian, looking puzzled. He'd changed into a sweater and held a newspaper, finger marking the place. Anyone would have taken him for someone enjoying the comfort of his own home.

As Clive angrily demanded an explanation, the other looked blank.

"Listen, mate," he said, "this is my apartment. I've lived here for years. And I've never seen you before in my life."

An hour later, at the local *préfecture de police*, Clive and Ellington gave their rival versions of events to the *juge d'instruction*, the magistrate who decides if a crime has been committed.

Ellington produced documents proving his title to the property. He referred casually by name to other tenants, none of whom Clive had yet met. Asked for evidence of his right to occupy the apartment, Clive had nothing. His copy of the lease, rent receipts, even his passport had been in the apartment, and were now either hidden or destroyed by Ellington. As for the agent who negotiated the lease, she was out of town and couldn't be reached.

Even as he explained this, Clive knew his story sounded improbable, even a little crazy. It was easier to believe that, as a newcomer and a foreigner, he'd spotted the empty apartment and "squatted" there. A few homeless people did this every winter, since the law forbade evicting even illegal tenants during cold weather, when they might risk their health by "sleeping rough."

Fortunately, Clive still had his cell phone. Among his anguished calls was one to Marie-Dominique and myself. Did we have any documents that might support his claim? Although it was by then one in the morning, Marie-Dominique drove to Montmartre to offer moral support while I burrowed among piles of papers until I found a letter addressed to Clive at the Montmartre address. Stuffing it into my pocket, I sleep-walked down an icy rue de l'Odéon to the deserted Boulevard Saint-Germain, and persuaded the lone cab standing at the rank to take me to Montmartre.

By now, Clive was close to panic. He had nowhere to live, no papers, no money, not even a change of clothes. Then there was Brutus. What had Ellington done with him?

He must have spoken some of these thoughts out loud, since the *juge* looked interested. Peering over his spectacles and, glancing from one man to the other, he asked, "Do I understand there is a cat?"

"Of course, *Monsieur le juge*," Ellington said easily. "He comes with the apartment. A house pet. He's been with me many years."

The *juge* nodded, then, meeting Ellington's eyes, said "So you will have no problem, m'sieur, in telling me this beloved animal's name."

Ellington's mouth opened, but nothing came out. There was a long pause. For the first time, his eyes held a whisper of panic.

By the time I got there, Ellington's deception was in ruins and the real story had begun to emerge. Behind in his mortgage payments and threatened with foreclosure by the bank, Ellington desperately needed to sell the apartment—impossible as long as Clive had a lease.

With the help of the agent, Ellington cooked up this deception. She would leave town for the weekend while he came from Australia, moved in, and swore he'd been there all along. With Clive out on the street and unable to prove he'd ever been a tenant, the agent could list the apartment at a sufficiently low price to guarantee a quick sale.

An hour later, a cell door closed on Ellington, prior to his ignominious deportation under threat of charges for theft and attempted extortion. Clive retrieved his possessions from where they'd been hidden, in the cave below his apartment.

As life returned to normal, Brutus reappeared from nowhere and rubbed himself against his leg. Clive served him an extra large portion of chopped liver, his special treat.

Only then did he recall that Montmartre's symbol was a black cat and that Rodolphe Salis believed them omens of good.

Was Brutus's role in this drama simply coincidence?

From his spot by the window, a pair of yellow eyes met those of Clive. Later he was never sure, but for a moment he could almost swear Brutus winked.

* · 3 · *

BUILDING BOULEVARDS

Modern Paris exists largely because of one man—Louis-Napoleon Bonaparte, otherwise known as Emperor Napoleon III, nephew of the more gifted Napoleon I. It was he who conceived a compact Paris tied together with wide boulevards, and hired the man who made it reality.

The emperor had his own reasons for reconstructing Paris. Convinced that the revolutions racing across Europe would soon reach France, he wanted both an imperial capital and a city easy to defend.

In 1795, his uncle, then a young general, faced a monarchist mob in the streets of Paris that outnumbered him eight to one. Not for the first time, Napoleon did the unexpected. Instead of risking his men in a bayonet charge, he loaded some cannons with canvas sacks filled with metal slugs, and fired into the crowd, scything down its members as machine guns would slaughter troops in 1914. The survivors fled—dispersed, wrote an admiring historian, by "a whiff of grapeshot."

Louis-Napoleon absorbed the lesson. If revolution came, grapeshot would solve his problems in the same way. But to rush artillery to the locations traditionally targeted by rebels—the presidential palace, the house of representatives, the town hall, the prisons—wide streets were needed.

To create these thoroughfares and the buildings that lined them, the emperor appointed, as prefect of the Seine, "Baron" Georges-Eugène Haussmann, a town planner sufficiently farseeing to visualize a modern Paris and ruthless enough to realize it. Haussmann demolished entire districts, replacing them with avenues lined with six-story apartment buildings, none taller than others in the streets on which they stood. These tree-shaded boulevards with wide sidewalks made Paris a city for pedestrians. Able to stroll without stepping into a puddle, mud, or something worse, people left their coaches and horses in the stable, and became *flâneurs:* men of fashion, free to amble around town. Watching them stroll by, merchants who had once sold tea, coffee, beer, and wine in bulk to be drunk at home now set up tables and offered samples of their products. The modern café was born.

The arrival of gas streetlamps, as well as earning Paris the title "City of Light," created another class of stroller.

Citizens of a clandestine Paris, the *noctambules* or night walkers only emerged when the bourgeoisie went to bed. To serve them, entrepreneurs stayed open later, turning their establishments into *cafés-concerts* or cabarets that offered music, dancing, or a floor show. With such attractive places to meet and talk, intellectual conversation, once confined to formal salons, migrated into the cafés. News of a new play or performer could reach every corner of the city in an evening. So could scandal. Naked gossip was across town before Truth could find its trousers.

The new freedom inspired such authors as Émile Zola, Honoré de Balzac, and Guy de Maupassant to explore topics once regarded as too shocking even to mention in public, let alone write about. Illicit love affairs and same-sex liaisons were discussed and pursued. Courtesans, gigolos, drugtakers, and swindlers rubbed shoulders (and other body parts) with the rich, beautiful, and talented in a society that soon became the envy of the Western world.

But in rebuilding Paris, Louis-Napoleon ignited the very revolution he feared. Haussmann gave no thought to the tens of thousands of slum residents made homeless by his reconstruction, any more than Napoleon I lost much sleep over the human cost of fighting wars. Both were, they told themselves, making history.

Many dispossessed slum dwellers settled in Montmartre. Already embittered, they became more so when the emperor provoked a pointless war with Prussia in 1870. Effortlessly, the forces of Otto von Bismarck overwhelmed his army, took him prisoner, and laid siege to Paris, battering its suburbs with artillery while systematically cutting off food and water.

Montmartre assumed military significance. It was perfect for keeping an eye on the enemy. "We seemed to be among the clouds," one visitor wrote. "Far below us lay the great shining city, spreading away into the distance; and although it was night, the light of a full moon and untold thousands of lamps in the streets and buildings below enabled us to easily pick out the great thoroughfares and the most familiar structures."

Even more usefully, the winds that turned its mills, blowing consistently from the north, could also carry hot-air balloons—named Montgolfiers, after their inventors, the brothers Joseph-Michel and Jacques-Étienne Montgolfier—over the Prussian lines. Loaded with military correspondence, journalists' reports, and, in one case, the minister of the interior, Léon Gambetta, they drifted hundreds of kilometers before the air within them cooled and they sank to earth around Tours or Poitiers. The mail, photographically compressed, was enlarged, and replies sent back to Paris via homing pigeon.

With the French army in disorder, the emperor a prisoner, the Prussians poised to take Paris, and the national government cowering in Bordeaux, at the other end of the country, Parisians turned for protection to its civilian militia, the National Guard. Seizing four hundred cannons, bought in part by public subscription, the Guard distributed them to working-class neighborhoods. One hundred and seventy of them went to Montmartre. As the Montmartrois lined up their artillery, ready to repel the Prussians, many reflected that such firepower gave them dominance over Paris as well. By the time the five-month siege ended, they were wondering whether rejoining the city that had rejected them was really worthwhile.

EATING ELEPHANTS

If Parisians felt the siege of 1870 more keenly in one sense than any other, it was hunger. The saying that only two missed meals in succession separate civilization from anarchy went double for Paris, where dinner has the ritual significance of a religious rite.

Once the cattle, pigs, sheep, and poultry were eaten, butchers turned to the next most common animal, the horse. For almost a century, it had been illegal to deal in horse meat, but the ban was lifted shortly before the war and the gilded horse's head, symbol of the *boucherie chevaline*, appeared once again. During the siege, Parisians ate an estimated 70,000 horses. Even the imperial court gave in, sacrificing a pair of thoroughbreds, a gift of Tsar Alexander II of Russia.

The poor made do with cats, dogs, rabbits, and rats. Rat sellers set up shop in the street, cheekily parodying conventional cooks by wearing the chef's classic apron and *toque*, and offering to butcher the rodent to the customer's satisfaction.

Just as even rats were getting scarce, the city's zoo, the Jardin d'Acclimatation, announced it could no longer feed its animals, and would, reluctantly, sell them as livestock. Butchers lined up to take advantage of this unexpected cornucopia of protein. The familiar went first. Antelope and other deer, whatever one called them, were still venison. Turtles made a classic consommé, and bear meat, correctly roasted, tasted like pork. But was armadillo edible? Aardvark? Anaconda? Who knew? One would have to buy them to find out, an expensive gamble.

Other decisions were less culinary than social. It seemed safest to leave lions and tigers alone. As for the apes, Darwin's *On the Origin of the Species* having been published in 1859, the better-read gourmets of Paris might hesitate to dine off an animal that could be a distant relative.

Monsieur Debos of the Boucherie Anglaise at 127 Boulevard Haussmann, who supplied many of the best right-bank restaurants, showed more imagination than his competitors. He snapped up the yak, reasoning that its hairy coat hid something like a buffalo, which could be eaten as beef. More audaciously, he also bought two elephants, Castor and Pollux. At 27,000 francs, they proved a bargain, since the tender meat of the trunks alone sold for 90 francs a kilo. Copious fat flowed from the marrow of their bones, and even their blood made a tasty *boudin noir* or blood sausage. On less exotic cuts, opinions varied. A journalist who had tasted camel, antelope, dog, donkey, and mule tried a *bifsteack* of Pollux but found it "tough, coarse and oily."

Preparing such exotic meats demanded a chef of exceptional talent. Alexandre-Étienne Choron of Voisin's restaurant rose to the challenge. A native of the northern city of Caen, one local specialty of which was tripe—cow's stomach—he wasn't fazed by some of the beasts he was required to cook. Elephant was his big success. Once Castor and Pollux were reduced to tusks and toenails, the management bought two more pachyderms put up for sale by the Jardin des Plantes.

Choron's 1870 Christmas Eve dinner for Voisin's wrote culinary history. Gourmets feasted on elephant consommé, followed by bear chops, roast camel, and kangaroo stew. Side dishes included a donkey's head and something called Cat Flanked by Rats. But there was more than great eating to this banquet. The printed menu was headed, pointedly, "99th Day of the Siege," a reminder that not even an army could stifle the French pleasure in a good meal.

An artist's conception of Debos's Boucherie Anglaise, 1871.

❋ · 4 · ❋

A TERRIBLE BEAUTY

THE COMMUNE

Like the student revolution of 1968, it's difficult to imagine Paris's 1871 anarchist revolt, known as the Commune, taking place anywhere but France.

In both cases, a few firebrands exploited a vacuum of power to launch an almost utopian plan for social transformation that, as even they must have known, was doomed to fail. Each initiative lasted only a few weeks. Once the government of the time got over its surprise, it crushed the uprisings with ease.

The Commune and *les événements* of 1968 differed most in their human cost. Uniquely in the history of revolution, not a single person died in the disturbances of 1968, whereas more than 20,000 were killed in the aftermath of the Commune, and many more imprisoned or deported. But as defeat is often more memorable than victory, the Commune lives on in legend. As W. B. Yeats wrote of the abortive 1919 Irish rising against British rule, out of such sacrifices "a terrible beauty is born."

On March 18, 1871, shortly after the siege ended and the Prussians, following a disciplined triumphal parade through the city, returned home, Generals Claude-Martin Lecomte and Jacques Léonard Clément-Thomas arrived in Montmartre with a company of troops to retrieve the 170 cannons supplied by the National Guard.

They never expected to be confronted by a group of local anarchists, least of all women. To add to their confusion, some, including their leader, Louise Michel, a schoolteacher known as "the Red Virgin of Montmartre," were dressed as men. Impatient with conventional gender roles, female Communards, in particular Michel, often wore male clothing, including the uniform of the National Guard. At a time when cross-dressing was so exotic that photographs of women wearing trousers were sold as pornography, this apparition was more alarming to the generals than the artillery they'd come to seize.

Michel argued that, having paid part of their cost, the people of Montmartre owned the guns. As voices were raised, the generals, forgetting that many of their troops

Communards admire their artillery, 1871.

were Montmartrois, ordered them to fire on the protesters. Not only did the soldiers refuse; they shot both generals, and joined the revolt.

As news spread of the insurrection, the National Guard freed Paul-Antoine Brunel, a supporter of jailed anarchist leader Louis Auguste Blanqui. Brunel led the Guard in a raid on the army barracks at Versailles, where the soldiers, leaderless, exhausted, and near starvation following the siege, surrendered without a fight. Escorting Jean Bellevois, leader of the Guard, to the deserted Hôtel de Ville, Paris's town hall, Brunel installed him in the office of the mayor, in effect placing him in charge of the city.

Brunel and other Communards urged the Guard to seize power and announce the birth of the world's first anarchist state, but the guardsmen dithered. "That evening we didn't know what to do," recalled one. "We did not want possession of the Hotel de Ville. We were very embarrassed by our authority." Desperate for leadership, they demanded the release of Blanqui from prison. When the government refused, the Communards took hostages, including the archbishop of Paris, Georges Darboy.

While the militants bickered, moderates elected a ninety-two-member Communal Council and began repairing the damage of the war and Napoleonic legislation. Church property was seized, and religious education halted. The windmills of Montmartre, traditionally owned by the church, were handed over to their operators. A ninety-day moratorium on all debt forced moneylenders to return the tools and household goods pawned by starving workmen. Factories whose owners had fled were reopened under worker control. Some reforms were touchingly domestic. Bakers, for example, were no longer required to rise in the middle of the night to guarantee customers a fresh baguette at breakfast.

Had the anarchists surrendered their artillery, they might have seceded from Paris and retained some independence.

The village, after all, was barely part of the city. As British journalist Sisley Huddleston pointed out, "Montmartre—the true, the old Montmartre—was completely cut off from the city. When its joyful citizens demanded that it be made a *commune libre*, an independent entity, they asked for something which in reality they already enjoyed."

Fatally, however, the factions occupying the Hôtel de Ville could never resolve the contradiction at the heart of the Commune: how could anarchy, a creed that rejected all forms of government, be adapted to govern? As they debated, the army recruited new troops from areas in the south that had no loyalty to Paris, and marched on the city.

As events turned against them, the radicals, in a futile gesture of retribution, shot their hostages, including Archbishop Darboy, and set fire to any buildings with Napoleonic connections, starting with the town hall. After that, they torched the Palace of the Tuileries, the seat of city government, which burned to the ground. Rumor blamed the fires on gangs of women called *pétroleuses*, who supposedly roamed the city with bottles filled with paraffin and petrol, an early version of the Molotov cocktail. Journalists claimed that the odor of gasoline hung over the boulevards. Although this was utterly untrue, many falsely accused *pétroleuses* were shot without trial.

Female Communards on the march.

The arsonists would also have torched the Louvre had
not the painter Gustave Courbet, appointed Delegate of

Fine Arts by the Communal Council, redirected their energy into more labor-intensive vandalism. He suggested they tackle the column on Place Vendôme erected by Napoleon I to celebrate his victories. A hefty piece of construction, its stone core was sheathed in metal melted down from captured cannons and molded into reliefs showing his various triumphs.

While the mob hacked at the column, Courbet opened the galleries of the Louvre for the first time to the public. He also urged the Commune to continue the annual group exhibition, the Salon, but under more liberal conditions that favored new and unconventional talents. This led, in 1884, to the establishment of a Salon des Indépendants, where the new generation of artists could show their work.

The Commune collapsed as suddenly as it began. Helped by traitors who led them through old gypsum mines into the heart of Montmartre, the troops from Marseilles easily defeated the National Guard. At perfunctory trials, people were convicted on little or no evidence. "In Paris, everyone is guilty!" snarled a prosecutor. About 20,000 died in mass executions. Thousands were deported to the penal colony of New Caledonia. Gustave Courbet, blamed for demolishing the column on Place Vendome, was ordered to pay for its reconstruction at the rate of 10,000 francs a month. The government never got its money. Aged only fifty-eight, Courbet died in December 1877, just before the first installment was due.

Instead of extinguishing the flames of rebellion, the failure of the Commune fanned them. Every victim became a martyr. Communard rhetoric helped ignite the 1917 Russian revolution. "The Internationale," a song composed by a Communard, Eugène Pottier, became the anthem of militant communism.

> Arise, ye pris'ners of starvation
> Arise, ye wretched of the earth.
> For justice thunders condemnation;
> A better world's in birth!

Louise Michel's speech at her trial summed up the Communard spirit. Daring the tribunal to shoot her as it had shot so many, she said, "Since it seems that every heart that beats for freedom has no right to anything but a little slug of lead, I demand my share. If you let me live, I shall never cease to cry for vengeance." Awed in spite of themselves, they withdrew the death penalty and instead sent her to Nouvelle Caledonia. She survived, and returned to France, where she died in 1905, having never laid down the red flag of the agent provocateur.

THE BASILICA OF SACRÉ-COEUR

THE CATHEDRAL OF THE SACRED HEART

Of the ten million people who visit Sacré-Coeur each year, making it Paris's second most popular tourist attraction after the Eiffel Tower, few know anything of its confused history.

In any other city, such a hill would be topped by a castle or fortress. Only Paris has a cathedral, albeit one built in an incongruous style that reflects the mixed motives that inspired it. Adding to the oddity, two equestrian statues flank the entrance, one of Joan of Arc, the other of Louis IX, the king canonized for leading the Seventh Crusade. The belligerence with which both flourish their swords sits oddly with the vision of a compassionate savior.

Of seventy-eight designs for the new cathedral, the judges selected that of Paul Abadie, who had already worked on restoring Notre Dame. Breaking with both classic church architecture and the bombast of Napoleon III, the Basilica of Sacré-Coeur sprouted domes more suited to Istanbul than Paris. Abadie also chose to build in travertine, a limestone that reacts with rainwater to make calcite, a natural whitener. Unlike Notre Dame, which needed repeated cleaning, Sacré-Coeur would remain always white.

Even before work began in 1875, the project had enemies. Some saw it as more imperial extravagance; Charles Garnier's grandiloquent opera house but without the music. Others compared the domes to turnips, and one particularly sarcastic opponent saw them as giant penises squirting onto the city below.

Old gypsum mines, some cavernous enough to accommodate a church on their own, riddled the ground under the cathedral site, forcing engineers to dig down more than forty feet to find bedrock. So deep were the shafts on which the building eventually rested, joked opponents, that even if they excavated all the earth beneath it, Sacré-Coeur would continue to stand as if on stilts.

Abadie died in 1884. Six more architects worked on the project before it was completed in 1914. In 1899, when money ran out, the church appealed to pilgrims. Gravures in religious papers showed an angel urging them, bags of coins in their hands, toward the still-unfinished building.

World War I delayed consecration until 1919. By

then, few remembered it had been meant as a monument to Archbishop Darboy. Instead, it was seen to commemorate all victims of the Commune, whatever their politics, and those of World War I as well. In a crowning irony, the courtyard in front was consecrated in 1975 to the memory of the archetypal Communard, Louise Michel.

An angel urges the faithful to complete Sacré-Coeur, 1899.

❋ · 5 · ❋

THE DAILY GRIND

THE MILLS AND MINES OF MONTMARTRE

As long as Montmartre remained outside the city limits, Parisians ignored it. Nor did its cowherds and millers take much notice of what went on in the seething ants' nest at the foot of the hill. One writer called Montmartre "a quiet, out-of-the-way village, to which few people climb. The buildings have a tumbledown air; they are old. The streets are narrow, twisting, and steep. They are roughly paved with cobblestones. There are great pieces of waste land on which grows grass and where dogs and children disport themselves." The description would apply, more or less, for five hundred years.

Aside from pilgrims trudging uphill to the shrines of Saint Denis, most visitors to Montmartre were drinkers, enjoying the cheap local wine, which was exempt from city taxes. Those selling it didn't bother with permanent premises but set up *buvettes* or *guinguettes*—open-air bars with perfunctory shelter from the weather.

Cafés and restaurants didn't appear until the late eighteenth century, most of them around the main square, the Place du Tertre. The oldest, La Mère Catherine, dated from 1793, and boasted of adding a new word to the language. On March 30, 1814, Russian soldiers, part of the force occupying Paris after Napoleon's defeat in Russia, shouted that they wanted something to eat, and *bystro*—quickly. Soon, "bistro" came to signify a café that served snacks. (Linguists argue that "bistro" might just as well derive from *bistrouille,* meaning coffee that had been *corrigé*— corrected—with a shot of cognac. La Mère Catherine preferred its version, which appears on a plaque attached to the outside wall. Print the legend. . . .)

The revolution of 1789 dragged Montmartre into the rush of history. Georges Danton, minister for justice before being purged by Robespierre and sent to the guillotine, made a point of holding meetings in La Mère Catherine to show he regarded Montmartre as part of Paris. While he did so, rowdier elements evicted the Benedictines from their abbey, demolished its more ecclesiastical portions, and declared what remained to be the new Hôtel de Ville or town hall.

Before the monks fled, they buried its collection of

La Mère Catherine, the world's first bistro.

sacred relics: bones and other body parts supposedly of Christ and his saints. As one such holy object must be embedded in the altar of every church or chapel before it can be consecrated, these had a practical value to the religious hierarchy. The revolutionaries, however, were more interested in the jewel-encrusted silver and gold reliquaries that enclosed them.

The abbey's relics included splinters said to be from the cross on which Christ died and a piece from His robe. They owned part of the jaw of Saint Denis, a tooth of Saint Berthe, fragments of the skulls of Saint Anne and Saint Ignatius, a bone from the arm of Saint Francis Xavier, two vertebrae of Saint Innocent, a tooth and part of the skull of Saint Fargeau, a rib of Saint Marguerite, a vial containing some of the blood of Saint Barbara, a piece of Saint Joseph's robe, the belt of Saint Marie-Madeleine de Pazzi, and the entire mummified bodies of Saint Florent, Saint Beatrice, Saint Valentin, and Saint Olaf.

Of course some, if not all, were fakes. But relics were generally presented by monarchs or aristocrats as down payments on immortality, greasing the eye of the needle through which, the Bible warned, few rich men passed en route to heaven. Not wishing to give offense, churchmen accepted each gift and left God to provide a provenance.

Even after the revolution, Montmartre wasn't officially

part of Paris. The fence known as the Wall of the Farmers-General ran along Boulevard de Clichy. Everyone bringing goods for sale in the city was stopped at a *barrière d'octroi* or revenue gate, and taxed on their load. This included the two main products of Montmartre's mills: flour and gypsum.

Also called alabaster, gypsum, a bone-white stone, softer than marble, had been quarried in Montmartre since Roman times. Although it deteriorated if exposed to the weather, it carved easily and was ideal for objects that remained indoors, such as tomb sculptures and portrait busts. In addition, gypsum, when baked, ground to a powder and mixed with water, became a tough, fire-resistant building material, marketed as Montmartarite or, outside France, Plaster of Paris, still the basis of modern drywall or Sheetrock.

Gypsum mining only ceased in 1860, leaving the butte riddled with tunnels and scarred by open quarries. Eugène Haussmann, busily transforming Paris, took one look and gave up. Not only had mining made many areas unsafe; its meandering streets, following tracks laid down over centuries by goats and sheep, ill suited his stately rows of apartment buildings. Instead, the locals, adapting the paths worn by miners to carry their loads down the hillside, built wide staircases lined with town houses, a solution that became one of the district's most distinctive features.

But if any building typified Montmartre, it was the windmill. Since the fifteenth century, they'd crowded the hilltop, exploiting the wind from the north to turn their grindstones. The oldest, known as the *Blute-fin* or fine grinder, belonged to the Debray family. As well as milling corn and wheat for flour, it crushed grapes for wine, flowers for perfume, and gypsum for plaster of Paris. Rue Blanche and Place Blanche—White Street and White Square— earned their names from the spillage of gypsum carts that left the cobbles and verges powdered white.

In 1809, the Debrays moved their mill lower on the city

The windmills of Montmartre.

side and opened a *guinguette* where, in addition to wine, they served galettes. The term covered anything baked, flat, and rich in butter, from cookies, tarts, and pancakes to the *galette des rois* or kings' galette, a pie of puff pastry filled with *crème frangipane*, traditionally eaten to mark the arrival of the new year, a reminder of the three kings who came in search of the baby Jesus. The Debray name disappeared, and the mill became known as the Moulin de la Galette.

When the Prussians besieged Paris in 1870, 20,000 soldiers attacked Montmartre, recognizing its strategic importance as an observation point for the French artillery. Three members of the Debray family died defending their mill. In revenge, the dismembered body of Pierre-Charles Debray was nailed to the sails. Its grindstones never turned again. Instead, the Debrays roofed over the mill floor to create a dance hall and *buvette*, leaving the old mill tower and sails in place as both monument and advertisement. Although they no longer made or sold cakes, the name Moulin de la Galette survived.

A visitor of 1903 praised

> *the spacious ballroom, remodelled and redecorated with green lattice and crystal chandeliers. The orchestra is the best of its kind in Paris. The floor is*

kept in perfect condition. Adjoining the ballroom is a quaint summer garden. A flight of wooden steps leads from the garden to the table-like rock above, crowned by the ancient windmill bearing the date 1256.

Following the up-hill passage of the entrance, the walls of which are patterned with flowers and garden scenes, we entered the great ballroom. What a brilliant scene of life and light! The floor was covered with dancers, and the girls were making a generous display of graceful anatomy. This was the one night of the week when, not tired out from the drudgery of hard work, they could throw aside all cares and live in the way for which their cramped and meagre souls yearned.

That the dancers, in particular the women, had regular jobs was something new for Paris. Traditionally, girls had lived at home, helping around the house or on the farm until they married. A few might go "into service" as maids, working essentially for a room and their meals. But once large stores and factories began employing women, a new female working class appeared, with money to spend, mostly on clothes and entertainment.

Vincent van Gogh, Pablo Picasso, Camille Pissarro, and Pierre-Auguste Renoir all found plenty in these parties and dances to inspire them. Renoir's 1876 *Dance at the Moulin de la Galette* captured the pleasure of boys and girls enjoying a sunny weekend break. Appropriate to the Moulin's new status, they wear their "Sunday best," the girls in striped cotton dresses, the men in the Panama straw hats so common among working-class Parisians that the suburbs where they lived were known as "Panam'."

While the dance hall and cabaret flourished, the mill itself deteriorated. In 1915, the Friends of Old Montmartre saved it from demolition. Moved to a more sheltered location lower down the butte in 1924, it was declared a national monument in 1939.

Dance at the Moulin de la Galette *by Pierre-Auguste Renoir (1876)*.

The Moulin de la Galette in a photograph from 1898.

THE MAQUIS

The north wind that drove Montmartre's windmills chilled the exposed side of the butte. In cold
weather, moist air piled up against the steep face,
cloaking its wooded slopes in a chilly fog.

The only building of any size on this side of the
hill was the Château des Brouillards. Dating back to
the seventeenth century, the grounds of this Mansion of Mists covered 7,000 square meters, most
of it overrun by the dense scrub called *maquis*.
Refugees displaced by Haussmann invaded the un-
used estate, first by planting vegetable gardens and
straggling vineyards, then building shacks with lum-
ber scrounged from sheds and fences. Unable to
afford metal fixtures, they improvised; for example,
sardine cans, hammered flat, became door hinges.

Artists fitted into the *maquis* as best they could.
Some rented studios in the Château des Brouillards,
among them Vincent van Gogh, Amadeo Modigliani,
Suzanne Valadon, her son Maurice Utrillo, and Pierre-
Auguste Renoir. His son Jean, later an important film
director, was brought up there, and reproduced the
area in his film *French Cancan*.

This nameless shantytown extinguished what

remained of Montmartre's rural charm. Burglary, robbery, and even murder were commonplace. Abortionists touted for trade as *faiseuses d'anges*—angel-makers, since aborted fetuses went straight to heaven. Shady pharmacists refined opium into morphine, the drug of fashion among the aristocracy. Courtesans and their clients often carried their own hypodermics, which could be custom-made in silver or platinum, and inlaid with jewels.

Bootlegging thrived. Slapdash home distillers of absinthe often failed to remove a poisonous alkaloid, thujone, that caused addiction and hallucinations, earning for the drink its nickname *la fée verte:* the green fairy. The army, which at one time had doled out the popular aperitif to its troops, was forced in 1914 to declare it illegal as a threat to the health of young men who'd be needed to defend the country in time of war.

Unhealthy and undisciplined, a nest of anarchy and crime, the *maquis* couldn't last. Late in the nineteenth century, the city began clearing it to create a new deluxe suburb, called optimistically by one bureaucrat "the Beverly Hills of Montmartre." Key to this plan was a new street, Avenue Junot, curving down and around the slope. A modern version of the Opera district, reserved for upmarket private homes, apartment buildings, and hotels, Junot's spectacular views and generously large building sites tempted architects to exercise their imaginations.

Periodically halted by a lack of money, then by World War I, the creation of Avenue Junot wasn't completed until the twenties. The result, however, was worth the wait. At No. 15, innovative Austrian architect Adolf Loos created a villa for Dada founder Tristan Tzara, who'd married into money and left the avant-garde behind. Sculptor Adolphe Thiers designed his own home at No. 27 and in 1927 also created the art deco mansion at No. 28 for fellow artist Louis-Aimé Lejeune. Over its back entrance, at 22 rue Simon Dereure, he added a small and elegant grace note: a relief of the sculptor at work.

The avenue's largest building was the Hôtel Alsina at No. 39, which became popular as a showbiz watering hole and movie location. It stood in for a pension, Les Mimosas, in Henri-Georges Clouzot's 1942 film *L'Assassin Habite au 21* (*The Killer Lives at 21*), and in 1968, François Truffaut used it for *Baisers Volés* (*Stolen Kisses*). During the occupation, Lucienne Boyer operated her nightclub Chez Elle in its basement, and in 1944, when Édith Piaf headlined at the reopened Moulin Rouge, she slipped away with her young co-star and lover Yves Montand to a room at the Alsina. If the Bateau Lavoir signified Montmartre's artistic survival, the Alsina represented its demimonde, determined not to be silenced, no matter what the risk.

Those nostalgic for old Montmartre bewailed each new development, but they were in the minority. The world had caught up with them. They could boast at least one victory, however. In 1932, the plan to build apartments on La Belle-Gabrielle, a tract of scrub on the north slope, near the Lapin Agile, nudged the Friends of Old Montmartre into buying the land. In 1933, two thousand vines were planted, and le Clos Montmartre became the district's only vineyard. The president of the republic attended the first *vendange* in 1934, but so, more importantly, did theater personalities Mistinguett and Fernandel. After that, the harvest became an annual event, a celebration not so much of the wine, which is only average, but of the old hard-drinking bohemian Montmartre.

A street in the Maquis district, about 1880.

�֍ · 6 · ✦

THE LADY OF THE
CAMELLIAS

In the 1840s, France's courtesans led Europe in fashion, inspired the greatest of its artists, and attracted the wealthiest men of the day as "protectors." Each season brought a fresh crop of young women from the provinces. Men-about-Paris browsed them as they might the latest racehorses, taking one or two out for a canter before choosing a favorite.

The women competed shamelessly, wearing the most revealing gowns, appearing unescorted at the opera, flirting with anyone who might help them, and trading sex for assistance. The archetype was Cora Pearl, mistress of the Duc de Morny, half brother of Emperor Napoleon III. At one of her all-male dinner parties, she had herself carried in by four husky servants on a silver platter, nude except for a garnish of parsley. As this, the main course of the dinner, was placed before her goggling guests, the lady lay back seductively and wished them, "Bon appetit!"

Having selected his plaything for the season, a man set her up in an apartment, complete with servants, one of whom acted as his spy to ensure she was faithful. Lavishing her with clothes and jewelry, he squired her to fashionable balls and soirées. When he tired of her, she was dismissed with a generous settlement, which, for the provident, bought them a shop or an advantageous marriage.

In this world of women enslaved to men, Marie Duplessis, as she renamed herself, stood out. A friend described her as "very slim, almost thin, but wonderfully delicate and graceful. Her face was an angelic oval, and her eyes had a caressing melancholy. Her complexion was dazzling." Unlike her rivals, she dressed demurely, always with her signature flower, a camellia, pinned to her dress. But her pallor disguised a fatal illness—tuberculosis.

Agénor de Guiche, heir to the title Duc de Guiche-Gramont, became her first protector. He found Marie's reticence charming. She played the courtesan's usual subservient role, but, at the same time, asked to learn how to read. Startled that a woman might possess a brain as well as a body, he had his grandmother teach her.

Not content simply with reading, Marie started her own salon, inviting writers and thinkers to spend an afternoon in conversation. Her wit and agile mind impressed such notables as the novelists Honoré de Balzac, Eugène Sue, and

Théophile Gautier. She was soon so much in demand that Gramont grudgingly agreed to share her. Accepting six more protectors, she allocated each one a day a week. Resignedly, the men collectively purchased a wardrobe with room for seven changes of clothing.

None of the seven realized there was an eighth lover. Neither wealthy nor famous, Alexandre Dumas was the illegitimate son of the man who wrote *The Three Musketeers* and *The Count of Monte Cristo*. In love with Marie, he persuaded her to live with him in the village of Saint-Germain-en-Laye, arguing that country air might slow the progress of her tuberculosis. She acquiesced, but when rural tranquillity bored her and did nothing for her illness, she returned to Paris. In a bitter letter of recrimination, Dumas broke off the relationship, admitting he'd lured her away simply to monopolize her company.

Marrying another protector, the Vicomte de Perregaux, Marie squandered so much of his money seeking a cure for tuberculosis, even experimenting with hypnotism, that he divorced her. By the time she died in 1847, visits to every spa in Europe had left her penniless. She died alone, except for a hired nurse, to whose hand she clung during the last days of her life. "That hand," wrote Théophile Gautier, "she quitted only for the hand of death." Mourners at her funeral, shocked that no money remained for a memorial, discreetly paid for the tomb where she now lies.

Dumas dashed off a novel called *La Dame aux Camélias (The Lady of the Camellias)* based on their affair. It wasn't a success until he adapted it into a play and the great tragedienne Sarah Bernhardt agreed to play the lead role of Marguerite Gautier. As a final act of revenge on the woman he'd loved, Dumas visited Bernhardt on opening night and, ostensibly to help with her performance, gave her the letter in which he renounced Marie. Buyers had discovered it while pawing through Duplessis's few possessions after her death.

Composer Giuseppe Verdi saw the long-running play in 1852, and was inspired to write *La Traviata (The Fallen Woman)*. Marie/Marguerite became courtesan Violetta Valéry, whose aria "Sempre Libera" ("Always Free"), in which she celebrates the joy of a life, however short, lived to the full and on her own terms, became one of opera's showpieces. More recently, Greta Garbo played Marie/Marguerite in the Hollywood film *Camille*.

Both Dumas and Duplessis are buried in Montmartre Cemetery, only a hundred meters apart. The tomb of Dumas, characteristically grandiloquent, is topped with his life-size effigy in marble. That of Duplessis, more modest, has no image, but in spring and summer is generally decorated with a few white camellias.

BLOOM WHERE YOU ARE PLANTED

"Of course the eighteenth is the best arrondissement in Paris," boast the Montmartrois. "Look how many people come here and never leave." It's a typically wry joke on the fact that Montmartre contains most of the city's graveyards.

Opened in 1825, the Cimetière du Monmartre, third-largest in the city, began as an abandoned gypsum quarry used during the 1789 revolution to dump the corpses of thousands executed on the guillotine. Among the celebrities buried there are the painters Degas, Moreau, Greuze, and Picabia and composer Jacques Offenbach, the king of light opera. Offenbach's "Galop Infernale" often accompanied the cancan, the most accomplished performer of which, Louise Weber, alias La Goulue, is also interred nearby. A few meters away are the graves of composer Hector Berlioz and Adolphe Sax, inventor of the saxophone, a facsimile of which decorates his grave. Dancers buried here include Ludmilla Tchérina, so charming in Michael Powell's film *The Red Shoes,* and Vaslav Nijinsky, a bronze statue of whom in his Harlequin costume from *Petrushka* sits disconsolately on the monument purchased by his choreographer Serge Lifar.

Centuries of wind and rain have erased the names on many tombs. Sometimes only the metal statues remain. Many life-sized and often stained deep green with verdigris, they resemble the cast of a historical epic awaiting an infinitely delayed cue. A copy of Michelangelo's imposingly bearded Moses keeps watch over the grave of Jewish philanthropist Daniel Iffla, while a life-size effigy of Polish soldier Miecislas Kamieński, killed at the battle of Magenta in 1859, half reclines on his tomb, already sitting up, as if ready to rejoin the front line.

The red porphyry tomb of novelist Émile Zola, topped by yet another bronze bust, doesn't mention that his bones lie elsewhere. Scorned during his lifetime as "the sewage of literature" for his realist novels about life among the working class, twenty-five times denied entry to the Académie Française, then forced to flee the country after his manifesto "J'accuse" protested the army's framing of Alfred Dreyfus as a spy, Zola was posthumously accorded France's highest honor: reburial among the nation's great in the crypt of the Panthéon.

Those who distinguished themselves in life by a tendency to misbehave find themselves in good company in this resting place. Among the most visited of graves is that of filmmaker François Truffaut, a Montmartre boy who inherited some of the district's famous *diablerie*. School dropout, juvenile delinquent, petty thief, and finally army deserter, he was rescued by film historian André Bazin. Under his tutelage, Truffaut became the most acerbic of critics, then director of *The 400 Blows*, *Jules and Jim*, and the archetypal tribute to filmmaking's frustrations and satisfactions, *La Nuit Américaine* (*Day for Night*).

The grave of dancer Vaslav Nijinsky.

THE MOULIN ROUGE

Paradoxically, the crimson sails of Montmartre's most famous windmill, the Moulin Rouge, are purely decorative. Looming above Place de Clichy, they turn only to advertise the cabaret below. As Jane Avril, one of its stars, remarked dryly, "The only thing ground by that mill was the tourists' money."

Since the 1850s, the building at 182 Boulevard de Clichy had housed a dance hall, La Reine Blanche (The White Queen). By 1885, it was notorious as a pickup spot and hangout for prostitutes. In *Bel-Ami*, Maupassant's leading character, Duroy, visits it with his thrill-seeking mistress. "She held tightly to his arm, scared and pleased," he wrote, "casting delighted glances at the whores and pimps."

In 1889, a new owner, Joseph Oller, banished dancing to the basement and turned the ground floor into a cabaret. The park behind the building became a *guinguette* with an outdoor theater, overshadowed by a plaster elephant bought at that year's Exposition Universelle. Inside the elephant, a tiny theater presented attractions too racy for general audiences, among them a demonstration of belly dancing by a Madame Zélaska. Overhead, *salons privés* were available for intimate assignations.

Advertised as "the First Palace of Women," the new Moulin Rouge admitted only men, and specialized in bawdy comedy. Its stars included Joseph Pujol, aka Le Pétomane, a virtuoso of the fart. He could imitate cannon fire and thunder, and play tunes on an ocarina linked by a rubber tube to his anus. His repertoire included such operatic arias as "'O Sole Mio," and even "La Marseillaise."

More scandalous still was the cancan (pronounced *con-con*). To the "Galop Infernale" from Offenbach's *Orphée aux Enfers* (*Orpheus in the Underworld*), dancers burst from

The Moulin Rouge's gala reopening, 1889.

the wings, whooping, turning cartwheels, flourishing their petticoats, and competing to be the most agile and acrobatic.

Oller and his manager Charles Zidler claimed the dance was born of a spontaneous *chahut* or uproar when prostitutes from the basement, hoping to flush some clients from the all-male audience, invaded the cabaret, high-kicking and lifting their petticoats to show off their legs. In fact, Zidler remembered similar disturbances in the tougher *bals-musettes* and reinvented the cancan for the cabaret, hiring dance hall veterans to teach his girls a repertoire of splits, kicks, cartwheels, and tricks such as the *porte d'armes*, in which the dancer lifts one leg vertically like a soldier shouldering a rifle.

As the *"quadrille naturaliste"* or *"quadrille excentrique,"* the cancan became a feature of the Moulin Rouge and soon spread to other cabarets, such as the Bal Tabarin. The more exhibitionist performers were stars overnight, in particular Louise Weber, known as La Goulue (the Glutton). She soon had competition from Nini Pattes-en-l'Air (High-Kicking Nini), Grille d'Égoute (Sewer Grating), and La Môme Fromage (Little Miss Cheese).

The Moulin burned down in 1915 and again in 1921, reopening each time larger and more gaudy than before. In 1923, the rebuilt cabaret introduced a restaurant, even more salacious sideshows, and a permanent in-house troupe of sixteen cancan dancers, called *quadrilleuses*. An American visitor in 1927 praised "a big, flashy revue here. 100 girls who do not wear even a bangle. A band plays in the foyer during intermission. Everyone leaves their seats, promenades and drinks. Also a roof garden on top of the building, and you can dine here. Also a naughty exhibition of oriental dancers. How tame by comparison is theater-going in America!"

The Moulin Rouge's cancan girls, 1923.

GET SHORTY

THE GENIUS OF HENRI DE TOULOUSE-LAUTREC

Successive novels and films of Montmartre during *la belle époque* have fixed Henri de Toulouse-Lautrec in the popular imagination as an expressionless, self-pitying midget in a bowler hat, frock coat, and carrying a cane, waddling down a cobbled street en route to the Moulin Rouge.

The cliché scarcely does him credit. Considering his afflictions, he was remarkably good-natured. He enjoyed dressing up, and was photographed in a variety of eccentric costumes. He accepted gibes about his stature without rancor. Once, as he left the Moulin Rouge, a joker pointed to his short custom-made stick leaning on a chair and said "Don't forget your *pencil*, m'sieur!" Lautrec smiled at the joke and didn't mention the cane's secret, a glass interior, always filled with cognac or absinthe.

Toulouse-Lautrec signed his name to Montmartre as surely as he added to all his work the entwined letters *HTL*, his version of the Japanese printmaker's pictograph. To this day, his images of cabaret stars and prostitutes float in ghostly superimposition over the strip clubs and sex shops of Boulevard de Clichy.

Except for an accident of birth, Henri should never have come anywhere near Montmartre. Born an aristocrat in the southwestern city of Albi, he expected to lead a life of privilege, perhaps dabbling in art as a hobby. His earliest paintings and drawings are of the hunt and the horses in his grandfather's stable; leisure activities of a gentleman.

Hopes of such a life ended in adolescence. His father, the Comte Alphonse Charles de Toulouse-Lautrec-Monfa, had married his first cousin. Their inbreeding resulted in genetic abnormalities in young Henri, including unnaturally brittle bones. His legs, broken in childhood, never grew again. An adult from the pelvis up, his legs remained those of a boy.

The Paris doctors whom his mother consulted could do nothing. Once his father abandoned the family in shame and despair, Henri, in constant pain, remained in the city, solacing himself with art, alcohol, and sex. Within a year, Rosa la Rouge, a red-headed singer at Aristide Bruant's cabaret Le Mirliton, had infected him with incurable syphilis. That, knowing he faced insanity and premature death, he nevertheless turned his back on despair to create great art says much about his strength of character.

Most artists lived in Montmartre because it was cheap, while Henri, not lacking funds, went there in search of subjects. He found them in its cabarets and brothels. At the same time, it was his good luck, and ours, that Vincent van Gogh introduced him to the palette of yellows, greens, and blues with which he and Paul Gauguin captured the richness of Provence—a rainbow of colors, exaggerated, in the case of Van Gogh, by the skewed perceptions of schizophrenia. Scorning the photographically exact style of Salon artists, Van Gogh quoted to Toulouse-Lautrec the advice of Gauguin: "If a tree looks yellow to you, paint it yellow. Instead of making a shadow blue, paint it pure ultramarine. These red leaves? Make them crimson."

While studying with Léon Bonnat, Fernand Cormon, and Émile Bernard, Lautrec encountered Japanese ukiyo-e woodcuts. Little respected in the West, these masterpieces first arrived in France as wrapping paper for porcelain, but quickly attracted the attention and admiration of such artists as Renoir and Monet.

Intrigued by the possibilities of printmaking, Henri mastered lithography, then supplanting etching and woodcut as the medium for making multiple copies. Instead of scratching an image onto a sheet of copper or cutting it into a block of wood, the lithographer spread ink on a polished slab of stone and pressed the paper to it. The new colors pioneered by Van Gogh suited lithography to perfection. For the first time, an artist could render accurately the vividness of theatrical costumes and stage makeup as they appeared under the intensity of gas lighting. As Van Gogh had made Provence blaze, Henri stole his fire to illuminate Montmartre. The butte was reborn in the public consciousness in a storm of violet, crimson, and green.

Recognizing that cabaret had found its laureate, Oller hung a Lautrec painting in the foyer of the Moulin Rouge and commissioned Henri to design its posters. A ringside table was reserved for his exclusive use. He often remained there, sketching and drinking, until dawn, then strolled to his printers, an incongruous figure in evening clothes among the laborers headed for work and housewives buying the breakfast baguette.

Of his twenty posters, most were for the Moulin Rouge and its stars Jane Avril, Yvette Guilbert, and La Goulue. Besides these, he created images of singer-composer Aristide Bruant, advertisements for both of Montmartre's avant-garde theaters, Théâtre Libre and the Théâtre de l'Oeuvre, covers for sheet music, literary magazines, and books about theatrical life. During a short visit to England, he even executed posters for confetti and a new brand of bicycle chain.

Posters were only part of his output. He also documented the lives of women in the district's brothels. Moving into a bordello, he would remain there for weeks, recording the daily lives of its inhabitants. One madame even commissioned a set of paintings for the salon where the women greeted their clients.

However, it was by multiples that Henri won instant celebrity. Where a painting might be viewed by a few hundred spectators at a gallery or by a handful of whorehouse habitués, his posters appeared all over Paris while the ink was scarcely dry. Collectors followed bill-posters around the city at night, waiting for their creaking handcarts to disappear around the corner before peeling his latest creation from the wall while the glue was still wet.

Mocked by the artistic establishment for his commercialism, Lautrec also had to endure insults from working-class colleagues about his noble ancestry. "The fruits of old family trees are generally weak and, though red, wormy inside," one of them sneered after his death, aged only thirty-six. "This artist of Montmartre belonged to an exhausted race, and was a caricature of it—weak, shrivelled, counterfeit." Henri might almost have agreed. Physically at least, he was no advertisement for the gentry. He blamed his father, for whom he reserved a dying curse. *"Le vieux con,"* he murmured with his final breath. *The old bastard.*

Henri de Toulouse-Lautrec in the costume of the clown Pierrot.

· 8 ·

NEW ROMANTICS

Removing the tax gates didn't eradicate the invisible frontier separating "decent" Paris from its disreputable neighbor. Scores of bars and cabarets lined Boulevard de Clichy like an army drawn up for battle, the have-nots confronting the haves across the former Place de la Barrière, now renamed Place Pigalle.

At holiday times, particularly around Christmas, a funfair took over the narrow garden island running down the center of the boulevard. For the rest of the year, it served as a "stroll" for prostitutes. Prostitution was legal so long as the women registered with the police and submitted to a monthly medical exam. Others worked in brothels, known as *maisons de tolérance*, but many more walked the streets.

A complex taxonomy ruled the world of those women who would become known as "streetwalkers." The elite were the *chandelles* or "candles," so called because they stationed themselves under a streetlamp. Next came the *marcheuses* or "walkers," and the *pierreuses* or "stonies," who often loitered near *vespasiennes*, public urinals. *Chandelles* and *marcheuses* took their customers to one of the *hôtels de passe* that rented rooms by the hour, but *pierreuses*, true to their name, slipped with them into the shadows of a vacant lot or building site.

Alarmed by the glacier of vice inching toward the respectable hotels and stores of the *grands boulevards* around l'Opéra, the gendarmerie launched periodic raids across Boulevard de Clichy into the roughest establishments—pointlessly, as it turned out, since, as the *flics* kicked down the front door, the prostitutes, pimps, dope dealers, and petty thieves disappeared out the back, melting away into a labyrinth of cellars and tunnels. In desperation, the council made it an offense for bars and cabarets to have back doors, only to backtrack after a few buildings caught fire, trapping customers without means of escape.

Acknowledging defeat, the landlords and the law withdrew to the downhill side of the boulevard, and dug in. New zoning regulations reserved these streets for private residences. Bars, clubs, cafés, and cabarets were strictly excluded. Among the first to buy homes in this area were former bohemians, hoping to acquire respectability without entirely turning their back on Montmartre and their old friends. They included Victor Hugo, author of

Notre-Dame de Paris (The Hunchback of Notre Dame), and painters Camille Pissarro, Claude Monet, Paul Gauguin, and Théodore Géricault. Art dealers Goupil et Compagnie moved their premises there in 1881. Theo van Gogh managed the office, helped for a while by brother Vincent.

In 1823, journalist Dureau de la Malle called this sedate new suburb "La Nouvelle Athènes" (the New Athens). He meant only to point out how many residents were philhellenes, enthusiasts for everything Greek, and supporters, like British poet Lord Byron, of Greece's struggle for independence from the Ottoman empire, but others suggested that a district boasting so many painters, writers, and musicians deserved comparison with ancient Athens, cradle of all the arts.

That so many gifted individuals admired Greece had the unintended effect of turning the word "Greek" into a compliment. Novelist Gustave Flaubert referred to sculptor James Pradier as "a great artist, a true Greek, the most antique of all the moderns; a man who is distracted by nothing, not by politics, nor socialism, and who, like a true workman, sleeves rolled up, is there to do his task morning till night with the will to do well and the love of his art."

The term "meritocracy" would not be defined until 1958, but it was already stirring in the Paris of the 1820s. For the first time, French society entertained the idea that a man or woman born neither rich nor noble might attain merit simply by what he or she created. While such people could never be considered entirely respectable, one could at least acknowledge them in the street, invite them to an afternoon salon, or even, conceivably, to dinner.

But not every New Athenian cared for the embrace of the bourgeoisie. Their model was Britain, a leader in the industrial revolution fast transforming Europe. French might be the language of diplomacy but most businessmen spoke English. So many Englishmen sampled the attractions of Montmartre that locals took to calling them *livres-Sterlingues* (pounds Sterling) and began to pepper their conversation with such Anglicisms as *snob, rosbif, milord, le smoking* (for evening dress), and *double-v.c. (*for lavatory). Distressed, the Académie Française convened a committee to weed out these interlopers.

British tailoring invaded France with the military uniforms of World War I. In 1921, a visitor lamented, "In the eighties of the last century, there was still a distinctive individuality about the Parisian's dress; now the men are dressed in very much the same way as Englishmen." Both men and women wore trimly cut, mannish outfits, in particular the *redingote* or riding coat. Frenchmen also adopted the bowler, known, from its stiff rounded crown, as a *chapeau melon* or cantaloupe hat. Many stores specialized in the sober British style. When serial killer Henri Désiré Landru was tried in 1919, he appeared so dapper in the dock that someone suggested the company supplying his clothes should advertise "In town and in court, M. Landru is dressed by High Life Tailors."

The New Athenians built their homes in the English style. They introduced porches and cast-iron balconies, tiled friezes, decoratively plastered ceilings, rose gardens, teahouses, and conservatories. Even the area's parish church, the Église de la Sainte-Trinité, flouted tradition. Instead of entering through a cemetery-like churchyard, worshippers crossed a tree-shaded park with lawns and a fountain, passing statues representing the cardinal virtues of Faith, Hope, and Charity. As for its rounded Romanesque windows and soaring central tower, among the tallest in Paris, with an incongruous clock embedded in it, conservatives sneered that it looked less like a church than a town hall.

At the heart of the New Athens was the Square d'Orléans. Designed by English architect Edward Cresy, the serene columns and white facades of its forty-six apart-ments and six artists' studios would not have been out of place on London's Regent's Park. In 1842, piano virtu-oso and composer Frédéric Chopin and novelist George Sand bought studios close to their friend, painter Eugène

Delacroix. Alexandre Dumas, author of *The Count of Monte Cristo* and *The Three Musketeers*, moved there in 1833. For a housewarming, he borrowed a neighbor's apartment, combined it with his own, and held a costume party for four hundred people.

One of the least typical members of the New Athens was painter Gustave Moreau, a leading member of the group known as les Fauves (the Wild Beasts). Preoccupied with religion and mythology, he created symbolist canvases that veered from ethereal to morbid: "chimeras, centaurs, dancing Salomés," wrote one nonplussed critic, cataloging his subjects. "Orpheus charming the animals, Jupiter and Semele, bleeding Christ, unicorns, mystical flowers, Galatea, Pasiphaë, Herod: far-off characters from sacred, unknown, and mysterious lands."

Determined that his work should be remembered, Moreau redesigned his home on rue de la Rochefoucauld as a museum, and bequeathed both house and contents to the nation, stipulating that it be kept exactly as he left it. One would expect no less from the New Athenians. If they agreed on a single value, it was the sanctity of artistic freedom. For the first time, artists asserted their independence from patronage and demanded the right to depict the world as they saw it.

GEORGE SAND AND FRÉDÉRIC CHOPIN

The Romantic movement had no more glamorous personalities than pianist Frédéric Chopin and Amantine-Lucile-Aurore Dupin, Baroness Dudevant, better known as the writer George Sand.

At eighteen, Aurore, her preference among her Christian names, married "Baron" François Dudevant—a title self-styled only, since he was illegitimate. They had two children, but in 1831, deciding she'd done her duty as a wife, Aurore announced she was embarking on a five-year "romantic rebellion." When the actress Maria Dorval wrote her a fan letter, Sand replied boldly that she hoped "to see you either in your dressing room or in your bed." The two were soon lovers. Determined to break into the male-dominated trade of journalism, Aurore, at the suggestion of her friend Marie d'Agoult, mistress of composer Franz Liszt, began dressing as a man and haunting the alleys of the Latin Quarter. Smoking cigars and buying drinks for the local riffraff, she wove their gossip into pieces for *Le Figaro*. Although no more than, in her words, "a newspaper mechanic," she was at least being published. Cross-dressing appealed to her, too, and even after leaving *Le Figaro*, she still wore trousers from time to time, while adopting the male nom de plume George Sand, under which she wrote a number of successful novels. Dudevant endured the humiliation until 1835, when he and Aurore agreed to separate.

For her male lovers, Sand preferred wimps: sensitive, creative, but preferably in poor health, so she could play nurse. One of her first, the poet Alfred de Musset, suffered from a congenital heart condition that would kill him at forty-seven, an end hastened by his taste for opium and absinthe. Affecting pink suits and a wan manner, he took gloomy satisfaction in writing about others who died young. In his epic poem *Rolla*, his hero lavishes his fortune on a beautiful prostitute, then takes poison. Henri Gervex created a scandal with his canvas of Rolla contemplating his nude mistress the moment before his suicide.

Deciding Italian sunshine would improve Musset's health, Sand took him to Venice, only to become bored and begin sleeping with his doctor. Furious, Musset returned to Paris and lampooned her in an anonymous pornographic novel, *Gamiani, or Two Nights of Excess*, the heroine of which indulges in the most extravagant depravity, including sex with an orangutan.

Seducing an ailing Chopin, Sand repeated the Musset treatment, whisking him away to Majorca, off the Spanish coast. In summer, the weather there could be idyllic, but midwinter rain and cold almost killed him. He insisted on having his favorite piano shipped from France but, almost as soon as it arrived, returned to Paris.

On Square d'Orléans, Chopin and Sand moved into separate studios, sufficiently distant so that both could work in peace. Eugène Delacroix painted an incongruously domestic joint portrait, she in a gown, sewing as she listens to him play. It never quite worked, and was later cut in two, the halves displayed in different museums.

They and their friends often met at the rue Chaptal home of Dutch painter Ary Scheffer, formerly court portraitist to the emperor Louis-Philippe. He also dabbled in politics but was so disgusted by the excesses of Napoleon III that he abandoned public life in favor of art.

Chopin died in 1849, aged only thirty-nine. Sand lived to a robust seventy-two, unapologetically passionate to the end. "Once my heart was captured," she wrote gaily, "reason was shown the door." (In the background, one can almost hear Chopin's despairing cough.) Sheffer's house became the Musée de la Vie Romantique, a monument to their relationship.

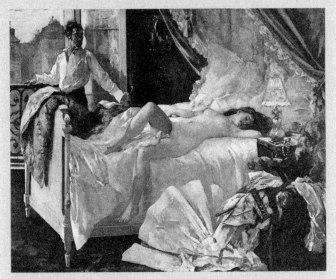

Rolla *by Henri Gervex, inspired by Alfred de Musset's poem.*

ARTISTS AND MODELS 1

ARTISTS

TOTALITARIAN REGIMES OFTEN RECRUIT ART IN THE battle for the hearts and minds of the people. France's nineteenth-century campaign was more subtle than those of Chancellor Hitler or Chairman Mao, but pursued no less energetically.

Aiming to increase the national respect for state and church, the government encouraged "history paintings." Panoramic and photographic in detail, these depicted episodes from the Bible, scenes from Greek and Roman antiquity, but above all military victories, particularly those involving Napoleon. Reproduced as lithographs, they found their way into every home, inspiring confidence in the administration and the army.

In return, the government rewarded such artists by buying their work to hang in public buildings, and awarding them lucrative contracts for murals. The wealthy hired them to paint their portraits and document their possessions: country châteaux, thoroughbred horses, prize bulls, dutiful wives, obedient children, and the occasional mistress.

They also received preferential treatment at the annual exhibitions or Salons, particularly that of the Royal Academy of Painting and Sculpture, a two-month show attended by at least a million people. Failure to be selected for the Salon could ruin a career. Even when an artist did make it past the hanging committee, he had to fight to have his work seen. In the so-called baroque style of display, paintings were hung one above another. Eye level was reserved for history paintings. Landscapes, street scenes, or anything lacking a moral lesson was exiled to the shadows near the ceiling. In the 1905 Salon d'Automne, the paintings of one group were shunted to a side gallery, where, a critic sneered, a Donatello statue already installed there appeared to shrink from the canvases as from savage animals. Stung, the artists, who included Henri Matisse, André Derain, Albert Marquet, Maurice de Vlaminck, and Kees van Dongen, defiantly christened themselves les Fauves (the Wild Beasts).

Salvation for the Fauves and other moderns would come from America, where nouveau riche industrialists collected art as proof of their new standing in the community.

The Paris Salon of 1787.

Unimpressed by history painting, they *liked* landscapes, city scenes, and nudes who looked like naked women, not Greek goddesses.

It took time for those agents and gallerists to emerge who could make the necessary introductions. Meanwhile, painters worked where they could, often trading canvases for food. Any buyer was pounced on. When Gertrude Stein expressed interest in a figure painting but found the legs unattractive, the dealer offered to have them cut off. The artist wouldn't mind, he assured her. "All he wants is the money."

Before he committed himself to art, Georges Braque

joined his father and grandfather in the family housepainting business. His knack for signs and lettering proved useful once he and Picasso developed Cubism since their canvases often used text—newspaper headlines; bottle and box labels—to evoke the urban world. René Magritte designed covers for sheet music, Raoul Dufy for wallpaper and upholstery fabrics. Suzanne Valadon modeled. Henri de Toulouse-Lautrec and Théophile Steinlen created posters, and for three weeks in 1900, Henri Matisse joined the ill-paid and overworked artisans decorating the pavilions of the Exposition Universelle. No disgrace attached to such menial work. It came with the territory. As a young man, Renoir painted flowers on dinner plates—work of which he remained sufficiently proud to hang some examples in his kitchen long after he became rich and famous.

Even when he was privately wealthy, an artist often embraced, as a gesture of solidarity, the frugal lifestyle of his friends. To hoard one's money was a betrayal of the bohemian ethic. Windfalls, as a point of honor, were splurged on drink and women. Amadeo Modigliani received a monthly allowance of 200 francs from his Italian family, but spent most of it on alcohol and drugs. When it was gone, he did sketches in the cafés for a few francs apiece.

Strikingly handsome, "Modi" habitually wore a corduroy suit, scarlet scarf, and wide-brimmed hat. Critical of

Pablo Picasso in Montmartre, 1904.

friends such as Picasso who dressed like laborers, he kept a furnished studio in Montmartre decorated with reproductions of Renaissance masterpieces. But the clothes soon became threadbare and, having lost the studio for not paying the rent, he slept on park benches or the floors of friends. Pneumonia complicated by tuberculosis killed him in 1920, aged only thirty-six.

For the artists of Montmartre, the breakthrough came

with the emergence of the dealers Ambroise Vollard and Daniel-Henry Kahnweiler. These men "got" the moderns. Vollard compared his first encounter with Cézanne's work in 1895 to "a punch in the stomach." Famously cranky, a hoarder who squirreled away hundreds of canvases in all but two rooms of his rambling twenty-three-room mansion, Vollard spent his last francs on the show that made Cézanne's reputation, and his with it. Recommending Vollard to his son, Camille Pissarro wrote, "I believe this dealer is the one that we've been seeking. He likes only our school of painting or works by artists whose talents have developed along similar lines. He is very enthusiastic and knows his job."

Vollard and Kahnweiler had the gambler's readiness to bet on their discoveries. In doing so, they created the international market for modern art, selling to clients whom established dealers would never have taken seriously. Mostly Americans, self-made, wealthy from mining, railroads, and oil, the new collectors had no artistic education, but made up for it with appetite. Rather than one painting, they bought dozens, transforming their homes into ad hoc galleries to display them. Some endowed museums where the public could share their pleasure. Modern art became fashionable, glamorous, and, for the artists, profitable.

Once money began to flow, those lucky enough to have

found buyers abandoned Montmartre. A few bought homes in the New Athens. Others joined the round-the-clock party that was Montparnasse, while a number relocated in Provence and along the Mediterranean, the route pioneered by Gauguin and Van Gogh, and further popularized by Cézanne, the most admired and influential artist of the period, who was a native of Aix-en-Provence. The unique southern light also seduced Bonnard, Matisse, Picasso, Chagall, and above all Renoir, who moved to the Riviera in his old age, both for the comfort its heat brought to his arthritis and for the light that illuminated his canvases.

Montmartre resigned itself to marketing its myth. As real artists left, forgers, con men, and eager amateurs rushed into the vacuum. Debasing the tradition pioneered by Modigliani, sketch artists overran Place du Tertre, badgering tourists to pose for a caricature. The Bateau Lavoir was restored, and plaques placed on cafés where Renoir or Van Gogh once drank. Former studios became museums, and streets were renamed to celebrate painters who, when they lived there, had been shunned.

THE BATEAU LAVOIR

No Montmartre studio space accumulated such a mythology as a former piano factory at 13 rue Ravignan. From the street, only a small storefront showed, but behind it the hillside fell away, making room for a building of three levels. Artists colonized it in the 1890s, dividing it into twelve studios. Poet Max Jacob, noting how the building swayed, creaked, and leaked in bad weather, like the hulks moored on the Seine where *blanchisseuses* took in washing, called it *le bateau lavoir*—the laundry boat.

Amenities were primitive. There was neither electricity nor heating. Water came from a well in the courtyard. The single lavatory was of the hole-in-the-floor variety. A market seller rented the lowest rooms, filling them with sacks of onions and carrots in summer and in winter sodden bags of mussels. Picasso's mistress and model Fernande Olivier described their studio in unflinching detail. "A rough bed on four legs in one corner. A rusty stove supporting a bowl of yellow china for washing; next to it, a towel and a bit of soap on a plain wooden table. In another corner, a poor little black-painted trunk provided an uncomfortable seat. A chair with a straw seat, easels, canvases of all sizes, paint tubes scattered on the floor, brushes, gasoline cans, a dish for making etchings, no curtains."

This squalor didn't deter a number of artists from living and painting there between 1904 and 1909, and from doing some of their most important work. It was here that Picasso and Braque developed Cubism, and Picasso completed one of the first important Cubist works, *Les Demoiselles d'Avignon*. Modigliani, Matisse, Dufy, and Utrillo all had studios there, as did Juan Gris, André Derain, Marie Laurencin, sculptor Jacques Lipchitz, and illustrator André Warnod.

Once the funicular railway opened in 1900, making it easier to reach the summit, writers and actors took to dropping in. The Bateau Lavoir acted as the moderns' embassy to the outside world. When dealers like Vollard and Kahnweiler needed to feel the cutting edge, this is where they came. Their influence was crucial. "What would have become of us if Kahnweiler hadn't had a business sense?" wrote an uncharacteristically grateful Picasso.

Once its artists moved on, the building deteriorated. After years of neglect, the government restored it in 1965, only to see it burn down the day it was due to reopen. It was completely rebuilt in modern style in 1970. Only a cabinet at street level displaying photographs of the interior in its original state offers a glimpse of the Bateau Lavoir as it was in its glory days.

The Bateau Lavoir.

·10·

ARTISTS AND MODELS 2

MODELS

NINETEENTH-CENTURY PARIS WAS THE GOLDEN AGE OF the artist's model. As sculptors and painters filled the salons with scenes from Greek and Roman mythology, men and women who could model for satyrs, gladiators, nymphs, and naiads never lacked work.

In 1880, 671 women between the ages of sixteen and twenty were registered as artists' models in Montmartre alone. Each Monday morning, dozens, some as young as six and many in costume, gathered by the pond in the middle of Place Pigalle, hoping to catch the eye of an artist. Elsewhere in the city, others congregated at the gates of the art schools, in particular the École des Beaux-Arts, hoping for work in its figure-drawing classes. In Montparnasse, where private academies clustered along rue Bréa and rue de la

Grande Chaumière, models were so numerous that they colonized an entire lane.

Many of these women were wives and daughters of the Italian masons imported to rebuild Paris. Having lived around art from childhood, they were comfortable with nudity, unlike women from other cultures, for whom modeling was one step removed from prostitution. Some Muslim and Jewish models struggled with the casual carnality of *bohème*. The favorite model of sculptor James Pradier came from a strict Jewish family. Seduced and abandoned by a lover and thus unmarriageable within her own culture, she took up modeling to support her parents, but the shame at exposing herself naked to a man not her husband, and, moreover, a gentile, drove her to a breakdown, and she died in a mental hospital.

A hierarchy existed among both male and female models. The elite, known as *modèles de profession*, worked only for established artists or the best schools and academies. "The perfect model doesn't need simply to be well-developed and in good health," a journalist explained in 1909. "He should also have been educated in mime, making him capable of modifying his expression and indicating character by the angle of his head. He must also be able to hold a pose for up to four hours, the usual duration of a session." Proud of their repertoire of poses, *modèles de profession* resented upstart artists who asked them to behave more naturally. When Édouard Manet complained to one man "Is this how you stand when you go to the market to buy a bunch of radishes?" he retorted indignantly that his poses had inspired more than one winner of the prestigious Prix de Rome.

Most new artists, unable to afford these professionals anyway, looked for subjects among ordinary people. Henri de Toulouse-Lautrec preferred prostitutes. "A professional model is like a stuffed owl," he said. "These girls are *alive*." Others used their girlfriends, creating a new category, the *modèle privilégié*—preferred models, typified by Amadeo Modigliani's Jeanne Hébuterne, and Picasso's Fernande Olivier and Françoise Gilot. Alice Prin, aka Kiki of Montparnasse, both modeled for and lived with a number of painters, among them Tsuguharu Foujita and Moïse Kisling, before falling for Man Ray, whose muse and companion she became until supplanted by the aggressive American Lee Miller. Suzanne Valadon also slept with numerous clients, including Toulouse-Lautrec, whom she tried to blackmail into marriage with a faked suicide attempt, and Renoir, who married another *modèle privilégié*, Aline Charigot.

Fernande Olivier, who lived with Picasso from 1905 to 1912, was not only his model and lover but also his housekeeper, his hostess when he wanted company, and defender of his privacy when he worked. Despite erecting a shrine to her in his studio at the Bateau Lavoir, Picasso was so jealous that, on leaving her alone, he would lock her in. The toll on these women was considerable. Alice Prin died an alcoholic and cocaine addict. The death of Modigliani so disturbed Jeanne Hébuterne that she leapt from a window, killing herself and their unborn child.

During the twenties, the model market was flooded by amateurs, mostly former *grisettes*—seamstresses, so named for their gray working dresses—or hatmakers, known as *modistes*. With the development of photolithography and the rise of illustrated magazines, many of these girls turned to pornography or prostitution, and a few to petty crime.

In one popular con, a guide, leading his American client on a tour of bohemian Montmartre, casually opened the door of an artist's studio, only to find him at work with a nude model. As the exasperated painter threw down his brush, protesting the interruption, and the guide apologized profusely, the model, taking her time, casually slipped into a peignoir and lit a cigarette. Unable to take his eyes off her, the flustered tourist often distractedly bought the daub on which the painter had been working. Once guide and client left, another painting was placed on the easel, ready for the next patsy.

Artists and models at play: the popular fantasy of Montmartre.

Stories of Paris's bold, free-spirited models circulated in the bars and smoking rooms of New York and London. Picked up and elaborated by illustrators, journalists, and screenwriters, they became the basis of a fantasy Paris that France's leisure industries covertly stoked.

Montmartre's big night for artists and models was the annual Bal des Quatz'arts or Ball of the Four Arts. Berry Wall, an American *bon viveur,* called it "a riot, a revival of paganism. It is also, in its way, a hymn to beauty, a living explosion of the senses and the emotions." Descriptions of its excesses filled the sensational weeklies for weeks ahead, and echoes of its depravity had Americans booking their holidays to coincide with the next event.

Begun in 1893 by the École des Beaux-Arts and initially held at the Moulin Rouge, the ball was reserved for students, models, and their friends, and then only if they arrived in costumes, the skimpier the better. The regulations explained that "the four ateliers [painting, engraving, sculpture and architecture] will be judged on the artistic merit and beauty of their *female* display." After some early scandals when naked women appeared as "living works of art," the police forbade total nudity. Instead, models and artists compromised with *le minimum*—a G-string, with quantities of jewelry and paint.

Attending the Bal des Quatz'Arts showed one truly belonged in *la vie de bohème*. Expatriates who succeeded in acquiring a ticket tried even harder than the locals to make an impression. Publisher Harry Crosby turned up in red body makeup, wearing a necklace of dead pigeons. Film director Luis Buñuel dressed as a nun, but was stopped at the door: his tickets were forgeries. In 1946, a reporter from *Life* magazine covering the first postwar *bal* was barred because of his conventional clothes. A sympathetic student guarding the door suggested he go away and come back in his underpants.

When the last Bal des Quatz'arts took place in 1966, Montmartre had long since ceased to be a center for art. All that remained was the bitter aftertaste, well articulated by

Jean Lorrain in his 1901 autobiographical novel *Monsieur de Phocas*. Lorrain's jaded hero bemoans a life frittered away in drinking, fornicating, sniffing ether, and smoking opium in the company of second-rate artists and their models.

"To think that I also have loved these maleficent and sick little beasts," he laments. "These fake Primaveras, these discounted Jocondes, the whole hundred-franc stock-in-trade of Leonardos and Botticellis from the workshops of painters and the drinking-dens of aesthetes. Their phosphorescent rottenness, their emaciated fervour, their Lesbian blight, their shop-sign vices set up to arouse their clients, to excite the perversity of young and old men alike in the sickness of perverse tastes! All of it can sparkle and catch fire only at the hour when the gas is lit in the corridors of the music-halls and the crude nickel-plated decor of the bars."

In response, hedonists might have quoted the apologia of Edna St. Vincent Millay for a life similarly misspent on the other side of the Atlantic.

> *My candle burns at both ends;*
> *It will not last the night;*
> *But ah, my foes, and oh, my friends—*
> *It gives a lovely light!*

SONS AND LOVERS

SUZANNE VALADON AND MAURICE UTRILLO

Like most Montmartrois, Suzanne Valadon came from somewhere else. She was only four when her father was sent to Devil's Island for counterfeiting, forcing Suzanne and her mother to relocate to Montmartre. Joining a circus, she worked as an acrobat and trapeze artist until injuries from a fall forced her to find another job. Since she had danced nude in private shows staged by the circus owner, Ernest Molier, modeling for artists was a logical next step.

Redheaded, sulky, and voluptuous, Suzanne was a *modèle privilégié* for Degas, Renoir, and Toulouse-Lautrec, among others. Renoir used her as a dancer in his triptych *Dance at Bougival* and as one of the nudes in *Les Baigneuses* (*The Bathers*). Exceptionally among models, Valadon also showed artistic talent and, encouraged in particular by Degas, became an accomplished painter of portraits and robust female nudes.

In 1891, she gave birth to a son. As any one of her clients might have fathered him, she took the boy around the cafés, inviting each to accept paternity. Most candidates ran for cover. Renoir, noted for his flesh tones, told her "It can't be mine; his color is terrible," and Degas, who excelled in painting ballet girls, protested, "I could never make such a baby. He's too lumpy." Finally a minor Spanish artist, Miquel Utrillo y Morhaus, volunteered. "I would be glad to put my name to the work of either Renoir or Degas!" he said.

Too busy to raise a baby, Valadon left him with her mother, who, like many frugal cooks, followed the custom of *chabrot*, pouring a glass of wine into the dregs of one's soup to float out the last morsels. As Maurice's adoptive father also drank heavily, by sixteen he was an alcoholic.

He also developed a morbid fascination with women—part lust, part fear. Encountering one in the street, he would tremble, whimper, and, if she fled, follow her, though always avoiding physical contact. Valadon, herself eccentric, wearing a bunch of carrots as a corsage and keeping a goat in the studio, to whom she fed her discarded sketches, resignedly placed him in a mental hospital.

This proved fortuitous, since the institution encouraged painting as therapy, and Maurice showed talent. Bringing him back to Montmartre, Valadon

Self-portrait of Suzanne Valadon, with mother, husband André Utter, and son Maurice Utrillo.

installed him in an upstairs room at her house on rue Cortot. To prevent him from sneaking out to get drunk, she locked him in, releasing him only for meals, which they always ate together in a restaurant. Rather than stifle his talent, she urged him to paint what he saw—which, for him, meant the streets outside his window. Those he couldn't see he copied from postcards. Providentially, illness imbued his canvases with a desolate beauty. Novelist Francis Carco praised their "leprous walls, livid skies, cold and mournful perspectives," a corrective to Renoir's sunny parties and picnics.

Utrillo's mental health improved with age. Married off to a middle-aged widow, he moved to the country, away from feminine temptations. His monument in Montmartre, appropriately, is a street, though an unconventional one; rue Maurice Utrillo is a cascade of stone steps, lined with town houses, running down the eastern slope of the butte.

11

ACTING UP

MONTMARTRE ON STAGE

Among the most incongruous of Montmartre sites is a tree-shaded square near the Abbesses Metro stop. A mural covers one wall of the park. It consists of a single phrase rendered 311 times in 250 different languages. The phrase? "I love you."

Even more improbably, the square is named for an artist of whom one person in a million has heard. Nor, in work or personality, did he celebrate the more tender passions. Quite the reverse. Jehan Rictus, the ultimate Montmartrois loner, was the very embodiment of misery.

The butte has never encouraged performance. Its few theaters are too small to seat a significant crowd. In the nineteenth century, most presented revues, though occasionally an adventurous entrepreneur, in a tradition continued by today's "off-Broadway" or the pub theaters of

London, staged one of the realist plays shunned by houses on the *grands boulevards*.

Between 1886 and 1897, the subscription-funded Théâtre Libre of André Antoine presented more than a hundred plays in the naturalistic style championed by novelist Émile Zola. In an 1880 essay, Zola attacked producers who would rather stage frothy comedies than a play like *Thérèse Raquin,* which he adapted from his own novel about an adulterous affair that ends in murder.

After failing to persuade his amateur group to produce one of Zola's plays, André Antoine formed Théâtre Libre, committed to presenting works by such playwrights as Ibsen and Strindberg, regarded as obscene for their treatment of infidelity, incest, and sexually-transmitted disease.

With no money for sets, he pioneered the open stage and theater-in-the-round; techniques which attracted the attention of theaters outside France. So few companies performed these plays that Théâtre Libre toured Europe, though never with sufficient success to stay solvent. At the end of its last tour, Antoine wrote disconsolately, "Here ends the odyssey of Théâtre Libre. Having set out seven years ago from my garret in the rue de Dunkerque with forty sous in my pocket to rehearse our first production in the little wine shop in the rue des Abbesses, I at last find myself in Rome, with almost the same sum in my pocket, surrounded by fifteen companions as dejected as myself, with a hundred thousand francs of debts awaiting me in Paris, and with no idea of what we will do tomorrow."

Other producers were more successful. At the Montmartre theater known as Théâtre de l'Oeuvre, the manager, Aurélien-Marie Lugné-Poe (the "Poe" was his own addition, out of admiration for the author of "The Tell-Tale Heart") specialized in the same realist plays as Antoine. In 1896, he also premiered the provocative absurdist *Ubu Roi* (*King Ubu*) by his friend Alfred Jarry. From the first word of the text, *"Merdre!"* ("Shit," plus an "r"), the theater was in an uproar. Though it ran only one night, the play and the word made both Jarry and the theater the talk of Paris.

Thanks to such showmanship, l'Oeuvre survived until 1929, attracting an often rowdy crowd, including police spies. Reporting on its 1893 production of *An Enemy of the People*, Ibsen's attack on the hypocrisy of local government that celebrates the courage of a "whistle-blower," one of these spies described the audience as "decadent poets and writers, long-haired and eccentrically turned-out aesthetes, ladies of the night who have graduated to 'the old guard': in other words the whole bohemian population of Montmartre and the area around the rue Blanche."

In contrast to the theater, Montmartre's cabarets flourished. At the equivalent of "open mike" nights like those common today in stand-up comedy clubs, the Chat Noir, Quatz'Arts, Lapin Agile, and others invited poets and singers to perform. Like middle-class intellectual folksingers of the sixties who culled their repertoire from plantation chants and Appalachian miners' laments, performers found that tales of misery and squalor got the best response, particularly when delivered in street slang. The most successful poets and singers wrote so convincingly in this style that audiences assumed they did so from experience, when in fact most came from privileged backgrounds.

Gabriel Randon, aka Jehan Rictus (a "rictus" is the fixed grin sometimes seen on the face of corpses), was raised by a part-English mother who aspired to act herself. Dropping out of school at seventeen, he lived briefly among bohemians and anarchists in Montmartre, memories of whom inspired *Soliloques du Pauvre* (*Soliloquies of the Poor*), an 1889 collection of poems in dialect and slang.

Théophile Steinlen's illustrations show Rictus as the apotheosis of gloom. Gaunt, unsmiling, with a long pointed beard and piercing eyes, he dressed entirely in black, including a top hat. "Very tall, very thin," wrote one reviewer of his stage presence, "with slender limbs, a flat beard, badly groomed, two drooping moustaches, eyes with reddened lids, a long coat flapping around his legs, his hands in his pockets, a speaking voice slow, sad,

Cabaret performer Jehan Rictus. (Théophile Steinlen)

mournful; thus Gabriel Randon, aka Jehan Rictus, recites his poems."

The brightest star of the Montmartre cabarets was Aristide Bruant, who had just as little experience of poverty as Rictus and even less of Montmartre. The son of a country landowner fallen on hard times, he worked as a railway clerk until, during his obligatory two years' military service, he met workingmen for the first time, and learned their slang. Preferring, as he put it, "the thugs and streetwalkers of the area" to his own class, he adopted a tough-guy persona and began playing the rougher cabarets of Belleville and Montmartre.

Bruant's material was as tough as his style was primi-

The king of bohemian Montmartre, Aristide Bruant. (Henri de Toulouse-Lautrec)

tive. Writing in the first person, he turned every song into a story. Each stanza ended with the name of the district where the story took place: "... *à la Bastille*," "... *à la Croquette*," or "... *à Batignolles*." In one of his most popular pieces, "À Saint-Lazare," a prostitute writes to her pimp from the Saint-Lazare women's prison. Diagnosed with a sexually transmitted disease during her monthly medical exam, by law she is locked up there until cured. But she thinks only of her "poor [Hip]'Polyte" and how will he be able to afford his little luxuries without her to pay for them, "because you're not the type who can go round picking up cigarette butts in the street." She even suggests he take on another whore—so long as he doesn't have sex with her.

Like Rictus, Bruant saw the value of a trademark costume: in his case a black corduroy suit, pants tucked into high black boots, a red flannel shirt, large black hat, long red scarf, and a clublike stick, all set off by a black cape. It signified no particular role, except the bully-boy persona that matched his verses. Once Toulouse-Lautrec created posters of Bruant in costume, both the outfit and the man who wore it became famous.

In 1885, when Salis's Chat Noir moved to larger premises. Bruant rented his two-room space on rue Rochechouart and launched his own cabaret. He called it Le

Mirliton, slang for a cheap tin whistle. Since the doors didn't open until 10 p.m., patrons had to queue up in all weather. In a tradition of Montmartre cabarets, they were mocked as they entered, either by Bruant or by his master of ceremonies. A sign above the door warned: "This is the place to come if you want to be insulted." After that, they were shoved together on uncomfortable benches and served beer at whatever price the management cared to charge. Bruant, as befitted a star, sang and recited only his own material, pausing to plug his sheet music, books, or the cabaret's magazine.

But audiences weary of ingratiating performers found this rudeness refreshing, and Le Mirliton flourished. It also made Bruant's reputation. Renaming it Cabaret Aristide Bruant, he hired a look-alike to perform his material while he played such fashionable *cafés-concerts* as Les Ambassadeurs and Eldorado. Even then, he continued to mock his admirers as a "pile of idiots who do not understand what I sing to them, not knowing what it is to die from hunger; those who have come to the world with a silver spoon in their mouths. I revenge myself in insulting them, in treating them worse than dogs." The illusion of his fabricated working-class persona survived until his death in 1925, when, true to type, he expired in a small house on rue des Saules (Street of the Willows), role-playing to the end.

AU LAPIN AGILE

A wooden shack, ancient and rickety, the Lapin Agile stands on rue des Saules, on the steep northern slope of the butte. Formerly the Cabaret des Assassins, it became Au Lapin Agile in 1880 when artist André Gill painted a new wooden sign showing a rabbit with a bottle of wine jumping out of a saucepan. People began to speak of "Gill's rabbit"—*le lapin à Gill*—which soon became Le Lapin Agile—The Agile Rabbit.

Customers today receive the same offhand reception as a century ago. No food is served, and the only drink is a cherry concoction of which each person receives a glass on entry. After that, they are crowded onto a bench around the walls and treated to a cappella performances of traditional songs, some dating back to the fifteenth century but most, like "Le Temps des Cerises," associated with the revolution and the Commune. Baffling to foreigners, these can be deeply moving to the French who know their history. In the words of singer-songwriter Claude Nougaro, a onetime performer there, "Le Lapin Agile is a strong-room in which eternity is preserved."

In between songs, a comic, speaking only French, works the crowd, continuing the tradition of insulting the clients. Once his antics have the customers laughing, he's likely to point out a group of grinning foreign tourists. "Will you look at these dumb Americans," he says conspiratorially. "Laughing like idiots when they don't understand a word I'm saying."

From its earliest days, owner Frédéric (Frédé) Gérard encouraged singers and poets to audition new material, sometimes accompanying them on guitar or cello. As The Frisky Rabbit, it even featured in the 1943 Hollywood film *Above Suspicion*. Fred MacMurray and Joan Crawford, as the price of their meal, harmonize on the sentimental ballad "A Bird in a Gilded Cage." Comedian Steve Martin also made it the setting of his 1993 play *Picasso at the Lapin Agile*, which describes an imaginary meeting there between Picasso and Albert Einstein.

Though Jehan Rictus and others did perform here, it was more popular as a hangout for painters, including Modigliani, Picasso, Utrillo, Derain, and Braque. In 1905, Gérard commissioned a painting from Pablo Picasso to decorate the main *salle*. In return, he wiped his drinking debts from the slate and gave him an unlimited line of credit. In the painting, called *Au Lapin Agile,* Picasso, dressed in the vivid patchwork costume of Harlequin, sits next to model Germaine Pichot while Frédé plays guitar in the background. Gérard sold the painting seven years later, but the canvas, along with others by Utrillo and Vlaminck, helped make the Lapin world-famous.

The Lapin Agile also attracted illustrators and cartoonists such as André Warnod, Roland Dorgelès, and Emmanuel Poiré, who called himself "Caran d'Ache," after *karandash,* a Russian word for pencil. Sporting the cloaks, wide-brimmed hats, and flowing hair of old-style bohemians, Warnod and Dorgelès conned drinks out of the more gullible visitors who wandered up the butte in search of "local color." The two were notorious jokesters. For the 1911 Salon des Indépendants, they created a canvas called *And the Sun Sinks Below the Adriatic,* supposedly the work of Joachim-Raphaël Boronali, an artist of the equally imaginary Excessivist school. As critics studied the yellow and green seascape with its smears of sunset crimson, Dorgelès distributed copies of the Excessivism manifesto. Impressed, a collector bought the painting for 400 francs. Once they'd milked the joke for all it was worth, Warnod and Dorgelès admitted that, while the seascape was their work, the crimson additions were made by the random slashes of a brush attached to the tail of Gérard's donkey Lolo.

A poet recites at the Lapin Agile, 1920s. (Frank Reynolds)

THE GHOST CABARETS

HEAVEN, HELL, AND NOTHINGNESS

For the first quarter of the twentieth century, no nocturnal tour of Montmartre was complete without visits to its "ghost cabarets," Cabarets du Ciel et d'Enfer (Cabarets of Heaven and Hell) and the Cabaret du Néant (Cabaret of Nothingness). All were on Boulevard de Clichy, the first two sharing adjacent buildings at Nos. 53 and 55, the third at No. 34. The same entrepreneur designed all three, financed by music hall star Georges-Henri Dordane, aka Dorville, who owned the site of Heaven and Hell, where he had previously operated a *café-concert*.

The ghost cabarets were a response to the growing numbers of foreign tourists to whom the comic songs and recitations of most *cafés-concerts* meant nothing. Dordane, borrowing from the circus and the carnival, imported elements of the fun house and the ghost train, and made creative use of the crypts and tunnels beneath the boulevard. Since the buildings themselves provided most of the entertainment, he could economize on staff. The only food served was sandwiches, so he needed no kitchen or chef, and as there was no dancing, he could get by without a full band.

Pigalle, not easily surprised, had seen nothing like these cabarets and their eye-catching facades. Plaster figures of gods and monsters leered and gaped, a motif carried on in the grotto-like interiors, where reliefs of either angels in ecstasy or souls in torment decorated the walls.

Customers who pushed through the black velvet curtains barring inquisitive passersby had to endure, in the style of Aristide Bruant, an insulting welcome from a master of ceremonies who, at the Néant, wore the costume of a *croque-mort* or undertaker. Most visitors took it with good humor, although British journalist Ellsworth Douglas suggested that anyone "touchy, thin-skinned or squeamish, [who] holds death in awe, or understands French too well," should look elsewhere for entertainment.

Having run the gauntlet of abuse, customers entered the Salle d'Intoxication, where chandeliers of human bones cast a feeble light on tables made from coffins. A waiter arrived to take drink orders. "Robed and cowled in black," wrote Douglas, "he will ask in lugubrious tones whether you will have Arsenic, Cholera, the Pestilence, or merely some fresh Sighs-of-the-dying." ("Cholera" was vermouth, "Pestilence" absinthe, and "Sighs-of-the-dying" a plate of sandwiches.)

Once everyone had a glass, the master of ceremonies dimmed the lights and lectured the customers about some paintings hanging around the room. All appeared innocuous until lamps were switched on behind them to reveal devils and other horrors menacing their nymphs and shepherds.

Following this, clients were offered, for a small extra payment, a visit to the Chamber of Disintegration. As sepulchral organ music droned, they filed down a tunnel into a dank crypt where a magician performed feats of transformation on volunteers from the audience. Wrapped in a shroud and placed in a coffin, a man was, it seemed, reduced in seconds to a skeleton. Other men who joined the magician onstage were made to appear surrounded by spectral witches, while women were menaced by a white-sheeted ghost; apparitions only the audience could see. Anyone familiar with music hall magic would have recognized "Pepper's Ghost," an antique stage illusion in which angled sheets of glass and directional lighting make objects and even people appear and disappear.

At the Cabaret d'Enfer, the drinks, except for their names—Molten Sins, Brimstone Intensifier—were identical to those at the Cabaret du Néant, as were the trick paintings in the bar. To accompany the lecture, a trio of devils seated in a cauldron, lit from below by theatrical hellfire, played eerie music.

Just as clients were thinking of moving on, an actor appeared in the costume of Satan. In medieval doublet, Mephistophelean beard, and brocaded cloak, he passed among the tables, selecting his victims. Spotting a pretty girl with her boyfriend, he paused by their table.

"Why do you tremble?" he growled to the girl. "How many men have you sent hither to damnation with those beautiful eyes, those tempting rosy lips?"

Then he rounded on her escort. "You will have the finest, the most exquisite tortures that await the damned. For what? For being a fool. For thus hanging upon the witching glance and oily words of a woman, you have filled all hell with fuel for your roasting."

As the couple giggled over all this attention, a robed waiter was at their side, suggesting a glass of Strychnine or even a bottle of Hemlock to help them recover.

The show at the Cabaret du Ciel was less sinister and the atmosphere more benign. A towering Saint Peter holding an enormous key delivered lectures on the delights of heaven. Drinks were served, wrote one visitor, by "seraphim in frizzy blonde wigs, crowned with roses, light wings attached to their backs, pink tights on their legs and espadrilles on their feet."

Then, as now, waiters made most of their pay from tips, which they were not shy in demanding. A client of the 1890s recalled how:

> one of the angel garçons sauntered up and gave us each a ticket admitting us to the angel-room and other delights of the inner heaven.
>
> "You are Eengleesh?" he asked. "Yes? Ah, theee Eengleesh arre verra généreux," eyeing his fifty-centime tip with a questioning shrug. "Can you make me un franc? Ah, eet ees dam cold in theese laigs," pointing to his calves, which were clad in diaphanous pink tights.

Only when they had been thoroughly fleeced were clients released to rejoin the crowds strolling along Boulevard de Clichy. Some may even have walked as far as the Taverne des Truands (Tavern of Gangsters) at No. 100, and, imagining it offered the same innocent fun, passed under the giant plaster effigy of a skeletal Grim Reaper wielding a scythe, flanked by menacing creatures cascading to street level. If so, they were in for a shock, since any resemblance to the more playful cabarets was superficial.

Several shady clubs had already occupied this site, among them the Running Pig, the Porcupine, and the Spider Music Hall, but the Taverne des Truands, opened in 1914, set a new low, despite starting with the best intentions. Tristan Rémy, a circus historian and member of the Dada brotherhood, launched it in the hope of reviving public interest in the skills of the circus. But jugglers and clowns attracted little attention, and it soon deteriorated into a clip joint, patronized by, according to one report, "pimps, coke-heads, morphine addicts, homosexuals, and whores."

Drinks were overpriced, and the only food served was "Proletarian Frites," a reminder of the "Bourgeois Frites" popular at the time of the Commune, when they were supposedly fried in the fat of the Communards' middle-class oppressors. As for the singers who replaced Rémy's circus performers, one reviewer observed they "obviously weren't concerned about censorship, because their songs were either nauseating or filthy."

The Truands preyed particularly on servicemen on leave. "When an innocent individual wandered into this establishment," warned one report, "a villainous maître d'hôtel lost no time in placing him next to a young woman who persuaded him to consume as many drinks as possible and, if he had a fat wallet, to spend the night with her in one of the numerous local hotels." Not surprisingly, the police closed it in 1916.

The ghost cabarets struggled once movies arrived and

other clubs began to offer more raunchy entertainment. In his 1931 story "Babylon Revisited," Scott Fitzgerald's protagonist, returning to the Paris he knew in the drunken *années folles*, notices that "the two great mouths of the Café of Heaven and the Café of Hell still yawned—even devoured, as he watched, the meager contents of a tourist bus."

Néant, Ciel, and Enfer survived until the fifties before becoming cinemas and supermarkets. The Taverne des Truands had an even shorter life. After World War I, it reopened as a puppet theater. When that failed, architect Charles Million was commissioned in 1922 to design a new facade and create an up-to-date theater in art deco style. As the Théâtre des Deux Ânes—Theater of Two Donkeys—it's still in business.

Salon of Intoxication at the Cabaret of Nothingness.

DYING FOR A LIVING

LE GRAND GUIGNOL

The one Montmartre scare show that delivered more than pantomime devils was situated, improbably, on the staid southern side of Boulevard de Clichy, in the heart of the New Athens.

The Grand Guignol, roughly translated as the Big Puppet Show, was the idea of Oscar Méténier, a police prosecutor turned playwright and crime novelist. In 1896, he staged a version of Guy de Maupassant's story "Mademoiselle Fifi," one character of which is a prostitute. Although prostitution was legal, a court judged the play obscene and shut it down.

Exploiting his notoriety, Méténier adapted some one-act plays from pulp novels he'd written for the series *Les Derniers Scandales de Paris* (*The Latest Paris Scandals*). To present them, he opened Le Grand Guignol in a former chapel at the foot of a cul-de-sac off rue Chaptal.

The Guignol might be Paris's smallest theater, with a mere 293 seats and a stage of only twenty square feet, but it was seldom less than full. Rape, torture, and violent death would always attract an audience, particularly when garnished with the most grisly stage effects; eyes gouged out, hands and fingers severed, faces seared with acid, or pressed to red-hot stove tops.

Promoted as "the world's most murdered woman," long-faced, wide-eyed Paula Maxa, born Marie-Thérèse Beau, was the Guignol's unchallenged star. The ordeals she endured on its stage, toted up by an admirer, included being "scalped, strangled, disembowelled, raped, guillotined, hanged, quartered, burned, dissected with surgical tools, cut into eighty-three pieces by an invisible Spanish dagger, stung by a scorpion, poisoned with arsenic, devoured by a puma, strangled by a pearl necklace, and whipped; she was also put to sleep by a bouquet of roses, [and] kissed by a leper."

A typical double bill began with *La Griffe* (*The Claw*), in which a number of women had their throats torn out by an attacker wearing a single black glove, disguising a hairy paw with jagged claws. The curtain-raiser, *Gai, Gai, Pendons-nous* (*Goody Goody, Let's Hang Ourselves*), was a black comedy. A new husband, unable to achieve an erection on his wedding night, tries to hang himself in shame, only to find that his attempt at self-strangulation induces the desired boner.

The Grand Guignol soon became an institution. Boxes were provided for those who preferred to relish pain in privacy, and prostitutes loitered in the lane outside, ready to satisfy clients who found the show unbearably exciting. Hollywood even borrowed the idea. In the 1935 *Mad Love*, Peter Lorre, in his first American film, plays a surgeon who spends every night at Paris's "Theater of Horrors," relishing the lovely Frances Drake tortured on the wheel.

The Guignol outlasted the ghost cabarets, only closing in 1962. By then, current events had eclipsed it. "We could never equal Buchenwald," said its last director, Charles Nonon. "Before the war, everyone felt that what was happening onstage was impossible. Now we know that these things, and worse, are possible in reality." Meanwhile, the term "Grand Guignol" entered the language as a synonym for any scene of bloody horror.

Poster for the Grand Guignol play L'Étreinte (The Grip), *probably around 1946.*

❋ · 13 · ❋

THE THREE PENISES OF NAPOLEON BONAPARTE

If a single characteristic separates the French and Americans, it is reverence for the past. To most Americans, history is yesterday's news. Not so for the French. To conserve its national heritage, known as *le patrimoine*, the French state pours billions annually into maintaining historic buildings, gardens and works of art, while, high on Paris's Left Bank, the Pantheon, a secular cathedral, preserves the remains of its most distinguished men and women. Above the colonnaded facade, an inscription reads simply: *Aux Grands Hommes, la Patrie Reconnaissante* (To its great men, their homeland shows its gratitude).

The French hold no man in higher esteem than Napoleon Bonaparte, the Corsican who became emperor of France and might have gone on to rule the world but for losing the battle of Waterloo, which his opponent, the

Duke of Wellington, conceded was "a damned close-run thing." Even his errors are revered. The abortive invasion of Russia is all the more respected for the scale of its miscalculation. Only a leader of truly heroic ambition could have come so grievously unstuck.

Among collectors of memorabilia, Napoleon is the gold standard. Former Italian premier Silvio Berlusconi, himself Napoleonic in both stature and ambition, slept in one of his beds, a canopied four-poster decorated with bronze eagles. Lesser enthusiasts compete to possess a letter signed by the emperor, a plate from which he ate, a piece of his clothing. Other souvenirs are less conventional. Four death masks are known, some including authentic strands of embedded hair, and no fewer than three collectors boast a shriveled piece of gristle, enclosed in a richly gilded frame, purporting to be the imperial penis.

The search for relics of Napoleon is the tip of a collecting iceberg. Known as *brocantes,* street markets of second-hand goods are a feature of life all over France. Sometimes called *marché aux puces* (flea market) or *grand balai* (big sweep-out), they are as integral to its culture as rugby football and the croissant. They range in size from the few dozen stalls of a *vide-grenier* (attic-emptier) on the edge of some Auvergnat village or a *vide-dressing* (vintage clothing sale) in Paris's trendy Marais district to the annual Grand

Braderie in the northern city of Lille, which, over a single September weekend, attracts three million people.

Brocanteurs generally leave the client to browse their tables without attempting a hard sell, but once a punter's attention is hooked, they pursue a sale with pit-bull tenacity. One dealer in military memorabilia tried to sell me an artificial leg, vintage World War I. Carved from beech, with steel fittings and joints, it did possess, I had to concede, a certain sinister charm.

"But what would I do with it, monsieur?" I asked.

Sensing a sale slipping away, he propped it upright, wooden foot planted flat on a tabletop.

"Perhaps," he said optimistically, "a lamp?"

CLIGNANCOURT

CITY OF STUFF

In Woody Allen's film *Midnight in Paris*, Owen Wilson and his intended in-laws visit the secondhand market quarter on the outskirts of Montmartre. It was an imaginative choice on Allen's part. America has yard sales and swap meets, Britain its car-boot sales, but though permanent secondhand and junk markets exist in other nations—Waterlooplein in Amsterdam, for instance—none approaches the scale of Clignancourt. Pronounced *Klin*-yan-kor, it's not a single market but an amalgamation of fourteen of them: Antica, Biron, Cambo, Dauphine, L'Entrepôt, Malassis, Malik, Le Passage, Paul Bert, Rosiers, Serpette, L'Usine, Jules Vallès, and Vernaison—each today a suburb in this metropolis of junk.

The market began when country merchants, rather than pass through the *portes d'octoroi* and pay city tax on their goods, sold them in fields just outside the walls. Around 1860, they were joined by the *chiffoniers* and *biffins*—ragpickers—displaced by Haussmann's rebuilding. The newcomers annexed nearby buildings, still remembered today for their original function: *entrepôt* means warehouse and *usine* a factory.

By the beginning of the twentieth century, Clignancourt was a cluster of covered arcades and paved lanes lined with stores selling everything from Rembrandt etchings and Boulle escritoires to cracked plates and worn-out clothes, the latter complete with the infestations that earned such places their name: *marchés aux puces:* flea markets.

Americans were among Clignancourt's earliest and most eager clients. In 1927, one of them called it "the funniest market in Paris. Here, all over the ground, is littered the strangest lot of junk. Old jewelry, silverware, pewter, old clothes, broken-down furniture, watches, dishes, etc. Anything can be purchased for a song." Softwood farmhouse tables and benches, worn hollow by centuries of use, sold particularly well. Professional dealers shipped them across the Atlantic by the boatload, where they were relabeled "Early American" or "Shaker" and priced accordingly.

For all its chicanery, the sheer diversity of Clignancourt wins over even the greatest skeptic. The protagonist of Diane Johnson's novel *Le Divorce,* a young American in Paris, initially dismisses it as "evidence of human materialism on a scale unimaginable to [her] before coming to France." Soon, however, she has become "accustomed to bronze panthers, plaster cupids, infinitely mended plates, hinges, mattresses, jeans, mirrors in their hundreds torn from the chimney breasts of all Paris, marble busts, torn canvases, chandeliers, seventeenth-century prints, deco lamps, things that cost thousands of dollars."

Age brought respectability to Clignancourt, formalized when the local municipality adopted it officially as Le Marché aux Puces de Saint-Ouen (The Flea Market of Saint-Ouen—pronounced Sant'Wen). Anxious to improve its image, the market cleaned up its act. Over the years, an army of amateurs, mostly Africans, had infiltrated the lanes. As some vendors panhandled and a few shoplifted, others spread blankets to offer junk that was dubious even by Clignancourt standards.

Ejected by the police. the newcomers took over the verges of every sidewalk within half a mile of the market. They're there still, more numerous each year. "Watch out!" warned a recent visitor. "Arriving at Boulevard Ornano, you cross a No Man's Land of swindlers, beggars, three-card trick merchants, pickpockets, sellers of telephone cards, smuggled cigarettes and every kind of forgery, all under the noses of the police, who do nothing."

But once you run this gauntlet, there are treasures to be found, some of them spiritual rather than corporeal. Woody Allen chose Clignancourt as the place where Owen Wilson's character begins to slip back into the Parisian past. A Cole Porter song on a scratchy 78 rpm is all it takes. As a character muses in Noël Coward's *Private Lives*, "Strange how potent cheap music is."

✻ · 14 · ✻

THE POPE OF THE CAFÉ

MONTMARTRE AND SURREALISM

THE SOLDIER IN THE NEUROLOGICAL WARD OF THE NANTES mental hospital was adamant: the war being fought in the mud of the Somme was all a show. Designers constructed the trenches and shell craters. They also strung the barbed wire, faked the explosions, even scattered corpses over No Man's Land.

A young therapist, André Breton, listened to this fantasy in bewilderment. Faced with events too horrible to contemplate, the soldier had created an alternative reality and taken refuge in it, as a child terrified by a nightmare pulls the covers over his head. But how could this uneducated *poilu*, literally "hairy one," as conscripts were known, invent something so intricate? Perhaps everyone possessed this capacity, but lacked the incentive to access it.

"I could spend my whole life prying loose the secrets of

the insane," Breton wrote. Demobilized in 1918, he moved to Paris, hoping to find the key that would open the alternative universe in all of us, creating "a revolution in the minds of men in which dreams and reality would fuse in a kind of absolute reality—*surreality*."

He wasn't the first to try. The Dada movement, founded in Zurich during the war, attempted to unlock the unconscious through play. Its members made poems by randomly picking words from a hat or composed them with nonsense sounds. "Dada means nothing!" boasted its founder, Tristan Tzara. Breton, briefly a Dadaist, wearied of their triviality. Taking the more serious members with him, he seceded to form the brotherhood of Surrealists.

Breton was an unlikely rebel. The son of a policeman, he habitually smoked a pipe and wore green tweed suits, with collar and tie. Neither drug-taker nor drinker, he disapproved of homosexuality and frowned on brothels. His moralistic manner earned him the nickname "the Pope of Surrealism."

As a first step to uncovering the marvelous in ordinary people, he opened a Bureau of Surrealist Research where everyone could record their dreams, but results were disappointing. The group turned to studying the drug-induced poetry of Baudelaire and Rimbaud, and the musings of Isidore Ducasse, a nineteenth-century mystic who styled himself Comte de Lautréamont. Ducasse's description of a boy "as beautiful as the chance meeting on a dissecting-table of a sewing-machine and an umbrella" suggested a provocative new style of language.

With his friend Philippe Soupault, Breton experimented with "automatic writing." Sitting opposite one another, they voiced their immediate thoughts, writing them down without editing or analysis. This was jazz with words—improvising with text, not music. Published as *Les Champs Magnétiques* (*The Magnetic Fields*), the results intrigued writers all over Europe, including James Joyce, who used the method to create Molly Bloom's soliloquy at the end of *Ulysses*.

In 1921, Breton moved to Montmartre, ordering members of the group to follow. Supposedly he left Montparnasse because of its "triviality," but his real motives were more conventional. In September 1921, he'd married Simone Kahn. Her large Montmartre apartment, close to Pigalle and Place Blanche, could house his collection of more than five thousand paintings, photographs, manuscripts, and folk art from Africa and the Pacific. It was also convenient to Brasserie Cyrano and Café Radio, both spacious enough to house meetings of the Surrealist brotherhood.

Known as *séances*, these took place between 6:30 and 7:30 each evening. Attendance was obligatory. (One of the few excuses for absence was that you had been having sex; so primal an urge should not be frustrated.) Generally Breton lectured. Occasionally he circulated questionnaires, including one on sexual habits, publishing the results in the group's magazine *La Révolution Surréaliste.*

After the meeting, he would usually dine with members of the inner circle. At one such dinner, following the survey of sexual habits, Breton asked poet Paul Éluard why his sexual encounters needed so much more time than others in the group.

"Well," explained Éluard, "one has to think of the partner's pleasure also."

"You can't be serious!" said Breton. "I never heard of such a thing!"

In lighter moments, they invoked chance with games like *Cadavre Exquis* (Exquisite Corpse), in which each person added a word or phrase to a sentence, without looking at what went before. The name came from an early success: "The exquisite corpse will drink the young wine."

Surrealism wasn't all talk. "The simplest surrealist act," wrote Breton, "consists of dashing down into the street, pistol in hand, and firing blindly into the crowd." No member tried this, but some used the movement's dislike of religion as a pretext to attack nuns and priests in the street. Occasionally, Breton led raids on productions by writers of whom he disapproved, particularly Jean Cocteau, or on anyone who misused the Surrealist name. They wrecked a café that dared to call itself Cabaret Maldoror and disrupted what German performer Valeska Gert advertised as an evening of "Surrealist Dance." Unfailingly polite, Breton always sent a letter of apology to the victim of the intervention, adding a spot of blood on the corner of the paper, proof that they too had suffered.

Breton's papal manner alienated many followers. When he forbade writing for money (it compromised spontaneity), many resigned rather than starve. Others left in 1927 when he decreed that all Surrealists should join the Communist Party. While not a problem inside France, such a declaration by a member living in Hungary or Romania meant, at best, prison, or even execution, as an enemy of the state. Many moved to Paris, joining others attracted by an urge as illogical as the young soldier's fantasy of a showbiz war. "There is absolutely no reason why [Benjamin] Péret came from Toulouse to join the group," says Jean-Claude Carrière, Buñuel's screenwriter and biographer, "why Max Ernst comes from Germany, why and how Man Ray comes from the States and Buñuel from Spain, and they all get together. There are probably billions of little *hasards* and coincidences. But something was calling them together. It was something they shared already before belonging to the same group."

A growing interest among visual artists saved Surrealism. Experimenting with the use of dreams and the subconscious, painters, photographers, and filmmakers achieved striking results. Surrealist art caught the public imagination as its poetry and fiction never had. People laughed at Man Ray's *Cadeau*, a flatiron studded with nails, Magritte's floating boulders, weightless as balloons, and his bowler-hatted heads with eyes, nose, and mouth replaced by breasts, navel, and pubic hair. Salvador Dalí's limp pocket watches, draped like fried eggs over bare tree branches, were as recognizable as the trademarks of Coca-Cola and Rolls-Royce.

Dalí became both the public face of the movement and the instrument of its downfall. A genius at self-promotion, he moved to the United States, where he painted celebrity portraits, worked with Walt Disney, Alfred Hitchcock, and the Marx Brothers, and graced the cover of *Time* magazine. When he began boasting, "I *am* Surrealism," Breton twisted his name into the contemptuous anagram "Avida Dollars"—hungry for money—but the damage was done. As a cuckoo invading another bird's nest topples out all rival eggs, Dalí's dreams crowded out those of everyone else.

But while Dalí hastened the collapse of Surrealism, history would administer the coup de grâce to both him and the movement. Surrealism, wrote art critic Peter Schjeldahl, "sprang from the spiritual wreck of Europe after the First World War and sank in the larger catastrophe of the Second." Even Breton saw its inevitable fate. Before his death in 1966, he complained to Buñuel, "It's impossible to shock people anymore."

THE RAZOR AND THE EYE

UN CHIEN ANDALOU

Even in the random world of the *Cadavre Exquis*, Salvador Dalí and Luis Buñuel made unlikely collaborators.

Dalí, the younger by four years, was slight, mercurial, impractical and sexually ambivalent; the opposite of burly, calm, competent, heterosexual Buñuel. They met at college in Madrid, part of a circle that included the charismatic gay poet Federico García Lorca.

After graduation, Buñuel left for Paris, ostensibly to work for the League of Nations but actually hoping for a career in movies. He found menial jobs on a few features and contributed film reviews to Spanish papers. Friends in Madrid believed he was on first-name terms with the cream of Paris's intellectuals, in particular the Surrealists, when he'd actually come no closer than glimpsing Louis Aragon and Man Ray in Montparnasse cafés.

With no movie career in sight, he decided to open a cabaret, and asked his mother for the same sum of money allocated to each of his sisters as their dowry. She agreed to give him the money, but not for a cabaret: gentlemen didn't run bars. It was only then that he thought of making a short film that would act as a "calling card" both to the film industry in general and to the Surrealists.

To help with the script, he recruited Dalí. Meeting in the Spanish town of Cadaqués, they composed a scenario using the same technique of free association as *Les Champs Magnétiques,* but with images, not words.

About the theme, there was no argument. Like all young Spaniards, the macho Buñuel and voyeur Dalí each struggled with a sexual guilt inflicted by their Catholic education. Sex, complained Buñuel, could be experienced by Spanish men in only two ways—in a brothel, or in marriage. Even when he married, the act remained burdened by shame. Before making love to his wife, he thrust a hatpin through the keyhole to thwart possible voyeurs, pushed furniture against the door to block intruders, then found further privacy in the bathroom. Both their sons, his wife confessed, were conceived in the shower.

Buñuel and Dalí first called their film, nonsensically, *Il est dangereux de se pencher au-dedans (It*

Is Dangerous to Lean Out the Window), an injunction that appeared in every railway carriage. During shooting, however, they had second thoughts.

It had been a college game in Madrid to puncture inflated reputations by writing insulting anonymous letters. In this way, Buñuel and Dalí attacked Juan Ramón Jiménez, author of the sentimental novel *Platero and I,* about a man's affection for his donkey.

Now their attention turned to Federico García Lorca. Their old college friend, an Andalusian, was winning international fame. At the same time, he offended Dalí by attempting to initiate him into anal sex. "I was extremely annoyed," said Dalí petulantly, "because I wasn't homosexual and I wasn't interested in giving in. Besides, it hurts!" Noticing that Pierre Batcheff, their leading man, resembled Lorca, Dalí and Buñuel renamed the film *Un Chien Andalou (An Andalusian Dog).* The insult wasn't lost on Lorca. "Buñuel has made a little film," he complained to a friend. "It's called *Un Chien Andalou* and I'm the dog!"

With the script written, Dalí remained in Spain, convinced his friend would never film it. But the challenge stimulated a new and practical side to

Buñuel. Calling in favors from actor Pierre Batcheff and cameraman Albert Duverger, with whom he'd worked on the Josephine Baker film *La Sirène des Tropiques*, and helped by his French fiancée Jeanne Rucar, who did everything from sewing the costumes to keeping track of finances, he was able to shoot the 17-minute film in ten days, and within its meager budget.

For the last days of filming, an angry and envious Dalí joined him in Paris. Tongue in cheek, Buñuel cast him as an actor in a key scene. As Batcheff struggles to approach a girl, he hauls two trainee priests, one of them played by Dalí, who are roped in turn to a pair of grand pianos in which are sandwiched rotting donkeys—a reference to Dalí and Buñuel's attack on *Platero and I*. To embrace the girl, Batcheff need only let go of the ropes, but the accumulated guilt and shame represented by the seminarians and pianos robs him of the will to do so.

The film's most memorable scene would remain the first. A young man, played by Buñuel, emerges onto a balcony at night, looks up at clouds sliding across the full moon, tests the edge of a straight razor against his thumb, then turns and draws the blade across a young woman's eye. Never has the imperative "Watch!" been more graphically conveyed. Even knowing that the eye is that of a dead calf did nothing to reduce its impact.

But was the film Surrealist? While Louis Aragon thought so, the only opinion that mattered was Breton's. Generally hostile to films that claimed to be Surrealist, Breton led the group in heckling a screening of Germaine Dulac's solemnly obscure *La Coquille et le Clergyman* (*The Seashell and the Clergyman*). He preferred the innocent Surrealism of commercial films such as knockabout Hollywood comedies and the gangster serials of Louis Feuillade.

In hopes of luring Breton into seeing *Chien*, Aragon presented it as the curtain-raiser to a private screening of *Les Mystères du Château de Dé* (*The Mysteries of the Château of Dice*), a short film commissioned from Man Ray by Charles de Noailles for the birthday of his wife Marie Laure. The invited audience received *Chien* with enthusiasm, but Breton, almost perversely, didn't attend. Instead, he waited for a public screening. Once he did see it, however, he recognized that Dalí and Buñuel instinctively understood the nature of Surrealism. Where Germaine Dulac evoked dreams with the use of slow motion and images softened by gauze and filters, *Un Chien Andalou* achieved the razor-sharp precision of nightmare.

Inviting Dalí and Buñuel to a séance at the Café Radio, Breton had each photographed in Paris's latest technological novelty, a Photomaton booth, then formally admitted them to the brotherhood. He could not have foreseen that while, in Buñuel, Surrealism would gain one of its most committed and faithful supporters, Dalí would come close to destroying the movement. No ironist, he might not have appreciated the joke.

Luis Buñuel in Un Chien Andalou, *1929.*

❉ · 15 · ❉

LE TUMULTE NOIR

O<small>N THE BUTTE, MORE THAN THE CATS WERE BLACK.</small>
Black faces were everywhere. Every year, more émigrés
from France's African colonies gravitated to Montmartre
and particularly its sister district to the east, Belleville.

American "minstrel shows" regularly played Paris,
usually with a mixed cast of African Americans, eked
out with a few white performers in blackface. Parodies of
plantation life in the Old South, these shows combined
sentimental ballads and comic songs with dances like the
cakewalk, sand dance, and the one-step. As much as the
public liked them, serious musicians didn't take them seriously—a situation that tempted the more adventurous
modernists, in particular Erik Satie.

Annoyed that Jean Cocteau's libretto for the 1917 ballet *Parade* included, against his will, passages for an air-
raid siren and tunes played on empty bottles, Satie wrote
a one-step into his score. Danced by Léonide Massine, it

caused a riot. "For the first time, music hall was invading Art-with-a-capital-A!" wrote young composer Francis Poulenc, who was in the premiere audience. "A one-step danced in *Parade!* When that began, the audience let loose with boos and applause." Following the performance, enraged dowagers advanced on Cocteau with needle-sharp hatpins. Guillaume Apollinaire, protected by his military uniform and bandaged head from a war wound, blocked their attack and, Cocteau believed, saved his sight, if not his life.

Jazz in strength was not long arriving in France. In 1918, as the first American troop ships docked, they were accompanied by a sixty-strong Marine Corps band of African Americans led by Lieutenant James Reese Europe. Formerly musical director for the dance team of Vernon and Irene Castle, Europe was charged with entertaining both American troops and the French public. His success with both was instantaneous, particularly when he played the one-step, a dance he not only claimed to have invented but described as "the national dance of the Negro race."

French audiences marveled at the apparent ability of Europe's sidemen to play complex unison passages without sheet music. In fact, all were accomplished sight readers, but as a concession to white audiences who preferred to think of African Americans as unlettered innocents, blessed with a "natural sense of rhythm," they performed their arrangements from memory, keeping the fantasy intact.

Black American musicians already working in France knew of this subterfuge but said nothing. So long as the French believed jazz was a skill unique to them, they would always be in work. Even when French unions forced impresarios to employ five local players for each foreigner they hired, producers preferred to pay a French band to sit backstage in silence rather than deny audiences *le jazz hot.*

Meanwhile, young composers experimented with other ethnic music, looking for a jazz equivalent that would be uniquely French. Darius Milhaud, one of the avant-garde group known as Les Six, returned from Brazil with a folk song called "Le Boeuf sur le Toit" ("The Ox on the Roof.") Entrepreneur Louis Moysés adopted the name for his Montmartre club, and Jean Cocteau, who played drums there, wrote a ballet of the same name.

Despite its jaunty Mexican-style rhythms, "Le Boeuf sur le Toit" didn't resemble jazz. Nor did the 1918 "Rapsodie Nègre," composed, tongue in cheek, by another of Les Six, Francis Poulenc. Allegedly inspired by the music of Madagascar and including a text by "Liberian poet Makoko Kangourou," Poulenc scored it for flute, clarinet, string quartet, piano, and baritone. Singers accustomed to Schubert and

Fauré protested at having to sing such texts as *"Pata ta bo banana loumandes / Golas Glebes ikrous / Banana lou ito kous kous / pota la ma Honoloulou."* At one wartime performance, attended by Poulenc, on leave from the trenches, the soloist, according to the composer, "threw in the towel, saying it was too stupid and that he didn't want to be taken for a fool. Quite unexpectedly, masked by a big music stand, I had to sing that interlude myself. Since I was in uniform, you can imagine the unusual effect produced by a soldier bawling out songs in pseudo-Malagasy!"

In 1925, Cubist artist Fernand Léger suggested to his friend entrepreneur André Daven that a popular show celebrating jazz might fill the 1,900-seat Théâtre de Champs-Élysées. The time seemed right. Jazz was in the air. The Exposition des Arts Décoratifs, then dominating most of the Seine's Left Bank, set out to promote French expertise in design but ignored music and dance. Milhaud's jazz-influenced ballet *La Création du Monde,* for which Léger created the costumes and sets, had been a succès d'estime, and Paris was filled with black musicians and dancers.

Daven took the idea of a jazz dance show to his backer, Rolf de Maré of the Ballets Suédois. De Maré approved but shared the common belief that only native African Americans could truly perform jazz. Rather than cast the show locally, de Maré and Daven contracted with New

York entrepreneur Caroline Dudley to assemble such a ballet, to be called *La Revue Nègre*.

Assuming Daven wanted the sort of show that had succeeded in the past, Dudley hired blues singer Maud de Forest and Spencer Williams, composer of such pop successes as "I Found a New Baby" and "I Ain't Got Nobody," to provide the music. Miguel Covarrubias's sets depicted Southern plantation scenes and docks along the Mississippi, in front of which the band would play while a chorus line of eight "Charleston Steppers" trucked and jived.

The last show to fill the cavernous Théâtre de Champs-Élysées had been Diaghilev's Ballets Russes in 1913, when the costumes of Léon Bakst and the decor of Alexandre Benois sent a tidal wave of innovation sweeping through every aspect of art and design. In particular, *Scheherazade*, with a bare-chested Nijinsky dancing the role of the Golden Slave, set a new standard of sex onstage.

La Revue Nègre, as assembled by Caroline Dudley, could not have been less like Diaghilev. Hoofers of greater agility and beauty than the Charleston Steppers were dancing in half of Paris's music halls. As for Maud de Forest, Paul Colin, the young artist hired to create a poster for the show, took one look at the aging and overweight singer, and dismissed her as "a washerwoman."

Daven agreed. Firing the director, he brought in local

African American choreographer Louis Douglas, known for his rubber-legged "Talking Feet" tap dance style. Douglas added himself to the cast and promoted clarinet virtuoso Sidney Bechet to front the band. He also bumped Maud de Forest from her headline spot, replacing her with the hottest dancer among the Steppers, nineteen-year-old Josephine Baker.

For Baker and another local dancer, Belgium-born Joe Alex, Douglas choreographed a hot new routine. When de Forest, furious at being pushed ever lower down the cast list, announced she was "indisposed" and would not appear on opening night, Douglas had a perfect excuse to feature Baker and Alex in "La Danse Sauvage." To ensure Baker was noticed, Daven and Rolf de Maré staged a preview for Paris's artists and socialites. Baker arrived on the arm of Paul Colin, the first European conquest of her busy sexual career.

As Douglas had hoped, Baker's first appearance on-stage, slung over the shoulder of the muscular, barely clothed Alex, created an erotic sensation to rival Nijinsky's Golden Slave. Janet Flanner, writing for *The New Yorker*, could barely contain her enthusiasm.

> *She made her entry entirely nude except for a pink*
> *flamingo feather between her limbs. She was being*

carried upside down and doing the splits on the
shoulder of a black giant. Mid-stage he paused,
and with his long fingers holding her basket-wise
around the waist, swung her in a slow cartwheel to
the stage floor, where she stood. She was an unfor-
gettable female ebony statue. A scream of salutation
spread through the theater. Whatever happened next
was unimportant. The two specific elements had
been established and were unforgettable—her mag-
nificent dark body, a new model that to the French
proved for the first time that black was beautiful,
and the acute response of the white masculine public
in the capital of hedonism of all Europe—Paris.

Flanner, an American and a lesbian, later admitted that
enthusiasm overpowered her critical sense. Among other
things, Baker was not black, but 50 percent white. Nor did
she appear entirely naked; the feather Flanner mentions
was attached to a G-string, *le minimum* for the Paris stage.

Neither a gifted dancer nor a spectacular beauty, Baker
had the intelligence and sense of humor to make a joke of
her sexuality. An exotically colored performer who not only
aroused both men and women but clowned as she did so
was something new to Paris. By the time *La Revue Nègre*
returned after its European tour, Baker could write her

Josephine Baker in her Montmartre club, about 1929.

own ticket—metaphorically only, however, since she was almost illiterate.

Leaving the show, she signed with the Folies-Bergère, which promised to build a series of productions around her—providing she submitted to a comprehensive makeover. While singing lessons improved her reedy voice, costumiers and makeup artists got to work on her body. Black might be beautiful, but brown was better. Helena Rubinstein lightened her skin with Crème Gypsy, a foundation that emphasized her natural coffee toning. Her eyes, outlined in kohl, became the most prominent element of her face. Brilliantine reduced her hair to a slick cap, parted in the middle. Every change drew even more attention to her comic rolling eyes and goofy grin. To complete the effect, Paul Poiret designed some abbreviated costumes, including one that became her trademark, a skirt of velvet bananas. Initially flaccid, the fruit became more perky and erect as her stage persona exaggerated a playful sexuality.

Recognizing a trend, every impresario in Paris wanted his own *Revue Nègre*. In 1929, Lew Leslie's *Blackbirds* revue ran for three months at the Moulin Rouge, featuring singers Adelaide Hall and Mabel Mercer, and dancer Bill "Bojangles" Robinson, who had toured with James Reese Europe in 1918.

With each new show, a few performers, as Baker had done, remained behind. Most gravitated to Montmartre. Sidney Bechet formed a band and played in many of its clubs, but the most prominent deserter from the *Blackbirds* was British singer Mabel Mercer, who linked up with another newcomer, former showgirl Ada Beatrice Queen Victoria Louise Virginia Smith, better known as "Bricktop."

BRICKTOP

After working as a boxer and drummer, Eugene Bullard, World War I's sole African American air ace, opened a tiny Montmartre cabaret, Le Grand Duc, on rue Pigalle.

With authentic jazz artists in demand, headliners were often lured away by offers of larger audiences and a bigger payday. In 1924, Bullard's star, Florence Embry Jones, left to start her own club, taking his clientele with her. Scrambling for a replacement, Bullard wrote to Alberta Hunter, whom he'd seen during a 1917 European tour. Instead, the next liner from New York brought one Ada Smith, a singer and dancer of whom he'd never heard, but who, according to gossip, had intercepted Bullard's letter and stolen Hunter's job.

Smith presented an odd appearance. Where, to quote a review of the time, "ivory-white, lipstick-red, and a suave, tawny brown are the colors of Florence Jones," Ada Smith's coffee skin, inherited from an African American father, clashed with the red hair and freckles of her Irish mother to create a cocktail of characteristics that attracted the slightly mocking nickname "Bricktop."

Langston Hughes, later a prominent poet of the Harlem Renaissance, was then doubling as busboy and barman at the Grand Duc. At his first glance, Ada appeared no competition for the flamboyant Embry, let alone the showstopping bravura of Josephine Baker. He described her "cute little voice, with nice, wistful notes. She danced a few cute little steps, tossed her head and smiled, and went around to all the tables and was pleasant to everybody."

Prodded by Bullard, the fashionable magazines announced her arrival, even if few had actually seen her perform: *Vogue* plugged her vaguely as "a pale, unspoiled beauty. She sings and dances like a star. She's young and new to Paris." By then, however, Langston Hughes, peering from the kitchen, had fallen under her spell. Revising his first opinion, he decided she was "a brown-skin princess, remote as a million dollars."

Bricktop helped put Le Grand Duc on the map. Fading movie star Fannie Ward, famous for her ageless appearance, had fled the intrusive probing of Hollywood lighting to open a Champs-Élysées beauty shop, The Fountain of Youth. Needing publicity at least as much as the club, she made the Grand

Duc her showcase. Her presence attracted an up-market following that included the then-Prince of Wales, soon-briefly-to-be Edward VIII, and, on occasion, Charlie Chaplin, T. S. Eliot, Pablo Picasso, Man Ray, Mistinguett, and Scott Fitzgerald.

Fitzgerald would boast, a trifle pathetically, of having discovered Bricktop before the man usually credited with igniting her European career, songwriter Cole Porter, but whoever deserves credit for making her his protégée, Porter's role was the more influential. He first learned of her in May 1926 when news reached him that Bullard's new singer included his songs in her repertoire. Famously touchy about interpretation, he paid an incognito visit in the early hours, to find Smith performing his "I'm in Love Again." Pleased by her version, he was even happier with her rendition of "Love for Sale," a small-time prostitute's weary lament. Any deficiencies in her voice were balanced by a lack of sentiment that matched the sophisticated lyrics.

The following night, Porter returned to ask, "Little girl, can you do the Charleston?" Versions of this dance, just then reaching Paris from New York, ranged from the staid to the acrobatic. Those who developed it were proud of its degrees of difficulty;

the lyrics to the tune to which it was most often performed, "The Charleston," boasted "buck dance and wing dance / will be a back number." Couples, rather than clinging to one another, often danced it side by side in unison. It could even be performed solo, which Ada did for Porter's benefit. Her agility dazzled him. Shouting "What legs! What legs!" he asked her to teach him the steps, and to do the same for his friends.

Bricktop gave Porter his first lesson in May 1926. Shortly after, he and his retinue moved to Venice for the summer, renting a palazzo, the Ca' Rezzonico, on the Grand Canal. Reserving a large domed barge belonging to the Excelsior Hotel, the most exclusive on Venice's Lido, he imported a black jazz band from Paris and hosted a summer-long party, mooring the barge next to each of the city's most famous sites in turn.

This disgusted the ailing Sergei Diaghilev, who'd chosen Venice for a quiet holiday. "[Porter] has started an idiotic nightclub on a boat moored next to the [church of Santa Maria della] Salute," he wrote. "The Grand Canal is swarming with the very same negroes who have made us all flee from Paris and London. The gondoliers are threatening to massacre all the elderly American women here. They are teaching the Charleston on the Lido beach. It's dreadful."

In charge of the Charleston classes was Bricktop, whom Porter had summoned by cable. "All Fixed For You To Give Lessons Excelsior Twice Week Let Me Know Date of Arrival Advise Auguste Will Engage Room." Her outspoken sassiness delighted him and his set. After she commented of the news photo of a man lynched in the American South that "*he* won't be wantin' no lunch today," he wrote for her the wittily funereal "Miss Otis Regrets," in which a butler explains that his mistress is unable to lunch since she's been hanged for murdering her lover. More spoken than sung, its *Sprechgesang* suited Smith's limited vocal talents.

As Bricktop's stocks rose, those of Eugene Bullard fell. Eased out of Le Grand Duc, he opened a new club on rue Fontaine, a narrow street running from the edge of the New Athens to the more raunchy Place Blanche. Called L'Escadrille (The Squadron), to trade on his flying reputation, it survived until 1939 when Bullard, who spoke German, learned of the impending war by eavesdropping on Nazi military officers drinking in the club. Fleeing to the United States ahead of the invasion, he ended his days as a New York city elevator operator.

Bricktop was featured at various Montmartre cabarets until 1931, when she took over the Monico, a big basement club at 66 rue Pigalle. Locals derided the idea of a luxury Montmartre night spot. Socialites and celebrities, they insisted, came to the butte for sleaze, not style. Moreover, in the wake of the 1929 Wall Street crash, high living was surely a thing of the past.

Smith didn't agree. Retaining the Monico's faux-Moorish entrance, she added her name and a photo portrait over the door, but completely refurbished the interior. To design it, she invited George Hoyningen-Huene, head of photography for French *Vogue*, whose fashion photographs and movie publicity stills defined the sleek modernist art deco style.

Her audacity paid off. So many guests attended her opening that some had to sit on the stairs. *The New Yorker* described "a mob of top hats and ermine flooding into the street." The decor inspired awe, beginning with the heavy curtains that blocked the entrance. Instead of the traditional velvet, Hoyningen-Huene chose black patent leather. Inside, a red carpet set off what one report described as "black-and-mercury glass tiles and black oilcloth, with concealed lighting in a white-wall ramp which, throwing heads and shoulders into silhouette, turns even drinkers into a charming decoration."

Once Bricktop's became, according to one magazine, "not only the newest but the smartest club to see or be seen in of all Montmartre," other cabarets followed suit. Those that couldn't afford expensive decor relied on novelty. At L'Arche de Noè (Noah's Ark), cages around the walls held stuffed lions, zebras, and giraffes. Le Plantation evoked America's Deep South with murals of the Mississippi and chairs upholstered in burlap coffee sacks. At Robinson, inspired by *Robinson Crusoe*, clients dined in elevated wooden huts thatched with straw, their meals winched up to them from the kitchen below. In the basement of 10 rue Fontaine, formerly Le Jungle, seashells and anchors decorated La Boite des Matelots (The Sailors' Club), one of a chain owned by Léon Volterra, impresario of the Lido, Olympia, and Folies-Bergère. Even the Boeuf sur le Toit inaugurated afternoon tea dances, while Place du

Tertre, at the heart of the old village, became a chic outdoor restaurant. Lamps hung in the trees, shining softly on women in evening gowns and men in *le smoking*, the shadows hiding the ancient cobbles that had known so much blood.

16

A VILLAGE OF SIN

MABEL MERCER LOOKED BACK ON BRICKTOP'S WITH NOS-talgia. "There was an elegance and beauty about it that doesn't exist anymore," she said. "People left their gold-and-diamond cigarette cases on their tables when they danced, knowing very well they would be there when they returned. It was a champagne world." Janet Flanner agreed. "As dawn came," she wrote, "there could often be seen in Bricktop's *boîte* Mme. Bricktop herself, the Lancashire singer Mabel Mercer, and the Prince of Wales, deep in mutually respectful conversation."

Not everyone remembered the club so fondly, nor its patrons as particularly honest. Cole Porter lost so many gold cigarette cases that he had "STOLEN FROM COLE PORTER" engraved inside each replacement. Smith complained she spent most nights at the cash desk, ensuring neither staff nor clients cheated her. Occasionally, she shared a drink with those guests in the back room who preferred not to be seen in public. Gangsters from Brazil, Argentina, or Mexico, known as *rastaquouères* or simply *rastas,* they ran the market in women and the newest fashionable drug, cocaine. Without their collusion, no club could survive.

For the unscrupulous, the hospitality trade was a gold mine. Graft began at the top. In 1898, César Ritz, manager of London's Savoy Hotel, along with its chef, the great Georges Auguste Escoffier, and sixteen kitchen staff, had been fired for taking kickbacks. Escoffier even set up a fake company to supply the Savoy at inflated prices. Unfazed, the men moved to Paris, where Ritz took over the hotel that still bears his name. Its cellars and larders were already well stocked with food and wine—paid for by the Savoy.

At the club and cabaret level, the same practices were taken for granted. In return for steering clients to specific brothels, gambling clubs, and dope dealers, headwaiters received tips from both the customer and the place they recommended. Liquor and food suppliers bribed barmen and chefs to use their products. Champagne vendors paid a bonus on each cork returned. Liquor was watered down, expensive brands switched for cheaper, or the size of shots reduced by slipping a celluloid disc into the measuring glass. And in this all-cash economy, nobody got the right change—if they got any change at all.

Sex was as energetically trafficked as food and drink.

Many clients arrived with a *poule de luxe* on their arm, while *entraîneuses*—literally "pullers"—worked the bar, coaxing men into buying high-priced cocktails or champagne. Every cabaret had a few gigolos, disguised as "dance instructors." The 1934 film *Wonder Bar* showed them preying on the American clients of Al Jolson's Paris club. Doing the tango with a lumpy matron, a svelte young man murmurs "You are so sweet, you remind of my mother," while, back at their table, a colleague enlightens her companion on the facts of Parisian life, explaining, "But of *course* you pay me, darling."

Ernest Hemingway was among Bricktop's clients, but not one of her favorites. He didn't dance, sulked if he wasn't the center of attention, drank too much, and, when drunk,

Lunch on Place du Tertre, 1923.

Dining on Place du Tertre, 1931.

picked fights. "A lot of people were raving about him," said Smith, "but I never took to him. He just wanted to bring people down, and he had a way of doing it, and he was liable to punch you at the same time."

She was closer to Scott Fitzgerald. Early one morning, the *préfecture* summoned her to bail him out. Wearing wet evening clothes and without identification, he was too drunk to remember his own name but could only mumble "Madame Bricktop." When she came to collect him, he explained that a manic Zelda had taken a notion to jump into a fountain, dared him to do the same, then fled. Back at the club, Ada opened a bottle of champagne and, sitting on the curb, drank it with him as his clothes dried off in the rising sun.

Looking back on those days in his story "Babylon Revisited," a sober Fitzgerald saw them in a less golden light.

> *He strolled toward Montmartre, up the Rue Pigalle into the Place Blanche. The rain had stopped and there were a few people in evening clothes disembarking from taxis in front of cabarets, and cocottes prowling singly or in pairs, and many Negroes. He passed a lighted door from which issued music, and stopped with the sense of familiarity; it was Bricktop's, where he had parted with so many hours and so much money. A few doors farther on he found another ancient rendezvous and incautiously put his head inside. Immediately an eager orchestra burst into sound, a pair of professional dancers leaped to their feet and a maître d'hôtel swooped toward him, crying, "Crowd just arriving, sir!" But he withdrew quickly.*
>
> *"You have to be damn drunk," he thought.*

GAY CLUBS

Once the 1789 revolution decriminalized homosexuality, same-sex relationships flourished in almost all of Europe. Britain alone maintained it as a crime, a law not repealed until 1967. Between the wars, many male gays, particularly from Britain, gravitated to Germany, where an athletic culture produced husky young men conforming to the homoerotic ideal. As author Christopher Isherwood put it, "Berlin meant boys."

Paris, more preoccupied with style, attracted those for whom dressing the part and playing the role mattered at least as much as physical gratification. Gay women gathered at the Saint-Germain mansion of railroad heiress Natalie Clifford Barney, doyenne of Paris's lesbian community. In the evening, they congregated at such clubs as Le Monocle, on Montparnasse's Boulevard Auguste-Blanqui. Male evening dress was de rigueur, ideally set off with a monocle.

Across the city, in Montmartre's rue Berthe, a glittering clientele of drag queens crowded Le Monocle's male equivalent, La Petite Chaumière (The Little Cottage). An American guide of 1927 dismissed it with a mixture of scorn and relish. "This is a place where men dress as women. Men of a certain degenerate tendency who infest every large city. If, however, you do want to see these Freaks cavort around and swish their skirts and sing in Falsetto and shout 'Whoops, my dear,' this is the place to see them."

Like most such descriptions, this one exaggerates and distorts. Far from parodying female roles, serious cross-dressers aimed to look, sound, and behave as much like women as possible. They were helped by a vogue for the *garçonne* or boy/girl style, for which women, not necessarily lesbian, adopted a unisex look, cutting their hair mannishly short and adopting male clothing. In *Un Chien Andalou,* sculptor Fano Messan, an archetypal *garçonne*, plays a mysteriously androgynous figure in women's clothes and cropped hair, clutching to her breast a severed hand.

Paris accommodated most sexual tastes. The urine-scented dark under the bridges across the Seine approximated the environment of London's "cottages," as public lavatories were known. Enthusiasts for sadomasochism gathered in the shelter of the colonnade opposite the Palais des Médicis, now the Sénat, alfresco sex was accommodated in a secluded area of the Tuileries gardens known as "Tata Beach," while the Bois de Boulogne, then as now, attracted exhibitionists and voyeurs. On warm nights, such wealthy sensualists as Harry Crosby and his wife Caresse would drive there with friends, park their cars in a circle, and enjoy group sex in the blaze of the headlights.

Jean Cocteau, who epitomized the city's gay scene, was not himself a cross-dresser. His tastes ran to watching young men washing themselves. Before the war, he'd been among the group who loitered in the wings of the Ballets Russes, ready to sponge down a sweat-soaked Nijinsky as he stumbled off stage after the exertions of dancing *Le Spectre de la Rose* or *Petrushka*.

Paris's public bathhouses accommodated Cocteau's preferences and those of his friends. The bisexual Louis Aragon confessed that the very word *bains* evoked "the thousand pleasures and maledictions to which our bodies are heir." One establishment created an early version of the two-way mirror, allowing Cocteau and other voyeurs to spy on their clientele. Another, frequented by both Aragon and Cocteau, offered private rooms, each furnished, in addition to a bath, with carpeted floors, framed paintings, a couch, and dressing table. Entering by one door, the customer locked himself in, then, after undressing, opened a second door onto a shared shower room where he could mingle with others in an atmosphere conducive to making new friends.

Gay lovers at a tango club. (Jean Dulac)

17

I REGRET NOTHING

ÉDITH PIAF

Few performers were less physically favored than Édith Piaf. Built like a boy, without, as she often lamented, either breasts or behind, she never topped four feet eight inches. Her few film performances were mediocre, not improved by gowns that mocked her birdlike arms and pipestem legs, making her resemble a little girl playing dress-up in her mother's clothes.

All these deficiencies became irrelevant once she sang. Alone onstage in a simple black dress, she could fill the largest hall with her voice. A simplicity of style amplified the poignancy of such songs as "La Vie en Rose," "Milord," "Sous le Ciel de Paris," "Hymne à l'Amour," "Padam Padam," and the autobiographical "Non, Je Ne Regrette Rien": anthems of abandonment, endurance, and despair.

Piaf was intimately associated with the street life of

Paris. "Her story is the stuff of working-class legend," wrote one biographer, "its joys and sorrows the material for her heart-stopping songs." Born in Belleville, Montmartre's sister village to the west—though not, as she sometimes claimed, delivered on the pavement under a streetlight—she inherited the diminutive stature of her father, Louis Gassion, who, only five feet tall, performed in the street as an acrobat and contortionist.

Abandoned by her mother, she lived with Gassion until the army drafted him in 1916. After that, she was taken in by her paternal grandmother, who ran a small brothel in Brittany. At fifteen, she joined her father in his act, initially passing the hat but later singing to attract a crowd. At a time when few people owned phonographs, street singers were everywhere, performing the latest hits and selling sheet music to be played at home. From them, Edith learned the tricks of the trade. Walls and courtyards served as natural amplifiers. She also gargled with coffee every morning to loosen her throat and increase the roughness demanded of every *chansonnier*. In winter, she and her girlfriend loitered around police stations and the barracks of the National Guard, hoping to be invited, in return for a few songs, to share their warmth.

Piaf was saved from the streets by a chance meeting with Louis Leplée, owner of an up-market nightclub just off the Champs-Élysées. Hearing her singing on a corner in Pigalle in 1935, he put her under contract and set about making her over. Forcing her to modulate her voice before it burned out, he commissioned new songs for her, notably from Marguerite Monnot, later known for the musical *Irma La Douce*. The plain black frock with which she would always be associated was his choice. It made her "La Môme Piaf," a brave little sparrow of the Paris streets. But in 1936, Leplée was murdered, probably in a dispute with Piaf's underworld friends over her contract. Suspected of complicity in the killing, she was questioned by the police but never charged.

New management dramatically raised Piaf's public profile. She was soon starring in every Paris music hall, as well as recording a succession of hit records and appearing in films. Her decision to continue performing during the German occupation maintained the momentum of her career. After the war, she played New York, and developed an international following. Even among people who spoke no French, her voice transmitted a passion that needed no translation.

Her tiny stature and persistently poor health did nothing to diminish Piaf's voracious sexuality. She blamed this on her early years living in brothels, where no woman ever refused a sexual invitation. Singers, actors, songwriters,

Édith Piaf.

and professional sportsmen shared her bed, but the love of her life was boxer Marcel Cerdan, briefly world welterweight champion. Abandoning his wife and children, Cerdan began a flagrant affair with Piaf, which ended in 1949 when the plane carrying him to meet her in New York crashed in the Azores.

Inconsolable, Piaf became more reliant than ever on drugs. Suffering from stomach ulcers, addicted to alcohol and, after injury in a car accident, to morphine, she continued to perform, even when her weight fell to sixty-six pounds. Collapsing in 1963, she lingered for months, semi-comatose, before dying, aged only forty-seven. Briefly reviving at the end, she voiced the classic epitaph of the Montmartrois. "Every damn thing you do in this life," she said, "you have to pay for."

THE WAR

The swiftness of France's defeat in 1940 and the subsequent Nazi occupation left the French dazed, particularly those in show business. Few French performers regarded Germany as an enemy. Most had German colleagues and a German audience. They toured one another's countries and collaborated on films and recordings. Producers often made films in two versions, with dual French and German casts.

Despite assurances that life under the Third Reich would continue as normal, Germany was soon draining France's strength and resources. The products of its agriculture and industry were diverted, and young Frenchmen due for their obligatory two years' military service were forced to serve it working in Germany factories.

In Paris, the German high command commandeered the best hotels. The Luftwaffe seized the Medici Palace, digging up the Luxembourg Gardens and planting vegetables. Designated a rest and recreation center of the Reich, the city was geared to providing entertainment for troops on leave. Most clubs, cafés, theaters, and brothels remained open, but under military control. Some served only Germans in uniform, while certain cinemas screened only German films.

Placed in charge of musical entertainment, jazz-loving Luftwaffe Oberleutnant Dietrich Schulz-Koehn guaranteed the safety of Jewish, Gypsy, and African performers as long as they played for the troops. To demonstrate his sincerity, Schulz-Koehn, who knew Paris well from before the war and counted many jazz critics among his friends, socialized publicly in full uniform with a group of black, Jewish, and Gypsy musicians. Reassured, Gypsy guitarist Django Reinhardt, France's greatest jazzman, who had been touring Britain when the Germans invaded, declined to remain there in safety and returned to Paris, where he played throughout the war.

While many writers and artists, including André Breton, Luis Buñuel, Antoine de Saint-Exupéry, and Marc Chagall, fled to New York, and a few actors and directors found work in Hollywood, singers and musicians needed an audience, ideally French. Most, after a minimum of soul-searching, worked under the occupation. Édith Piaf took refuge in the zone controlled by the puppet Vichy government but soon became bored playing to provincial audiences. "Krauts or no krauts," she announced, prior to returning home, "the capital of France is Paris."

Josephine Baker, exploiting the Italian connections of her lover, a fake Italian count, acted as courier for the resistance, work for which she was honored after the war. She was in the minority. Many French actresses, among them Mireille Balin, star of *Pépé le Moko*, and Léonie Bathiat, aka Arletty, took German lovers. Bathiat found no contradiction in this. "My heart is French," she said, "but my ass is international."

Maurice Chevalier remained in France, and even performed in Germany, albeit for French prisoners of war. Piaf did the same, as well as touring Vichy France. In Paris, she sang at the Moulin de la Galette and Salle Pleyel, but also in Le Chabanais and Le Sphinx, deluxe brothels transformed into nightclubs for the Nazi high command and its collaborators. In 1941 she made her film debut in *Montmartre-sur-Seine*, a sentimental story that exploited her working-class image and associations with the district. She played a flower seller, too much in love with an indolent but glamorous loafer to recognize the musically talented young man who adores her. Nothing in the film's sunny depiction of the butte suggests a city under occupation.

While stars found it easy to continue performing, lesser talents struggled. Gays were forced to wear a pink triangle on their clothes, and despite the reassurances of Schulz-Koehn, many musicians of borderline ethnicity were deported by the gendarmerie and Vichy's paramilitary police, the Milice. Cabarets closed as Germany drained them of essentials: staff, electricity, food, and, most precious of all, freedom of movement, restricted by a nightly curfew.

In Montparnasse, the great cafés boarded up their windows and doused their lights. In Montmartre, a few smaller clubs survived. One of these, Chez Elle (Her Place), occupied the basement of the Hôtel Alsina on Avenue Junot. "Elle" was smoky-voiced torch singer Lucienne Boyer. Accompanying her on piano was composer Georges van Parys, who also wrote the melancholy "Complainte de la Butte" ("The Lament of the Butte"), used in Jean Renoir's *French Cancan*.

Boyer lived daily with risk. Not only was she married to Jewish crooner Jacques Pills, Jean Neuburger, who, as "Jean Lenoir," composed many of her successes, including her theme song "Parlez-Moi d'Amour," was also Jewish, and his music therefore banned from public performance. By posting a "Jews Not Admitted" notice at the door of the club, Boyer hoped to be overlooked by the Germans. Nothing, however, could stifle her Montmartrois love of risk. Novelist Patrick Modiano celebrated the first New Year's Eve of the occupation at Chez Elle. "That night," he wrote, "Lucienne Boyer proved she was a star. Just after announcing the new year, she sang a forbidden song—'Parlez-moi d'amour.'"

After the war, Piaf and Chevalier denied having collaborated. Jewish friends testified that Piaf had sheltered them, while former prisoners of war explained how they used souvenir snapshots taken with her to forge ID cards. A handful of performers were blacklisted, even imprisoned. When Arletty was needed to re-record dialogue for *Les Enfants du Paradis*, the police brought her to the studio in handcuffs. But she was soon working again, while Chevalier and Piaf became more famous than ever.

❋ · 18 · ❋

LIBERATION

Paris emerged from the Nazi occupation as from a bad dream. The city was close to physical collapse, its fabric crumbling from neglect. In such ancient districts as the Marais, walls leaned and damp-rotted plaster fell into the street. Jerry-built workshops and garages invaded the stately courtyards of seventeenth-century palaces. Since almost nobody lived there any longer, most buildings in the Marais had become warehouses. When Le Corbusier urged the area's replacement with towering *unités d'habitation* rising from spacious parks, many voiced their approval. Only the partisanship of such lovers of old Paris as de Gaulle's minister of culture Andre Malraux staved off wholesale demolition.

Throughout 1946, the French indulged in an orgy of recrimination. Marshal Pétain, the World War I hero who led the collaborationist government, was sentenced to death for treason, but died in prison. Women guilty of "horizontal collaboration" with the Germans were publicly humiliated by having their heads shaved. More prominent collaborators, including Coco Chanel, fled the country; others were imprisoned; a handful committed suicide. The authorities executed a few, but many more were quietly murdered by their neighbors; killings to which the police turned a blind eye.

A few artists cautiously explored the complexities of occupation and collaboration. Published clandestinely in 1941, Jean Bruller's novel *Le Silence de la Mer* (*The Silence of the Sea*), written under the pseudonym "Vercors," probed a French family's hostility toward the sympathetic German billeted with them. In Marcel Carné's 1946 film *Les Portes de la Nuit* (*The Gates of Night*), a survivor of deportation stalks the man who informed on him.

The Communists, leaders in the resistance, expected to be rewarded with victory at the postwar polls. Instead, they battered ineffectually against the imperturbable Charles de Gaulle, the wartime leader-from-exile who rose above party divisions to become prime minister, then president. He dismissed the possibility of a Communist France with a sneer. "How can a single party govern a country which has two hundred and forty-six varieties of cheese?"

One of the Communists' few victories was to close France's brothels, bringing to an end the long-standing system of police-supervised *maisons closes* and *maisons de tolérance*. On paper, the initiative was a dream proposal, offering to ordinary voters the luxury of feeling virtuous about outlawing something they seldom, if ever, used. Led by Marthe Richard, a national heroine who had spied for France during World War I, the campaign ostensibly aimed to turn the buildings into first-time homes for young veterans—again something everyone could cheerfully support. In practice, however, few couples cared to begin married life in a former whorehouse, while the end of police registration and regular health checks for prostitutes brought back the old evils of pimping, streetwalking, and sexually transmitted diseases.

Depressed by the squalor of postwar Paris, young Parisians embraced the United States and everything it stood for. Under the occupation, a group called les Zazous had tried to imitate the style of Harlem's pimps and hipsters. Unable to replicate the baggy tapered trousers and long draped coats of the "zoot suit," they compromised on drooping jackets in plaids and checks, set off with a single incongruous accessory: a furled umbrella.

Postwar teenagers, lacking the leather jackets, jeans, and T-shirts seen in magazines and films, also assembled a uniform from anything that looked vaguely American: in their case lumberjack shirts, black cotton trousers, and tennis shoes, topped in winter with a loose sweater or duffel coat. The Zazous had danced to smuggled 78 rpm records or big-band swing broadcast by Armed Forces Radio. The new hipsters, jiving in the cellar clubs of Saint-Germain and Pigalle, preferred live New Orleans jazz of the kind popular before the war. They called their dancing "bebop," although it would be years before true bop, pioneered by Charlie Parker and Dizzy Gillespie, arrived in Europe.

If these people had a ruling passion beyond that of having a good time, it was the ascetic philosophy developed by Jean-Paul Sartre that he called existentialism. Few, if any, of his professed admirers had read Sartre's writings, or, if they read them, understood his ideas. For his part, Sartre disowned his groupies. In a notice posted at Le Divan, Saint-Germain's most fashionable bookshop, he declared "that band of check-shirted youngsters who haunt St. Germain-des-Prés [and who] came to be known as Existentialists bear no relation to me, nor do I to them."

While politicians wrangled and quasi-existentialists jived, Montmartre, with characteristic practicality, returned to work. Place de la Barrière was renamed for a former resident, the eighteenth-century sculptor Jean-Baptiste Pigalle, best remembered for chaste classical figures and cute babies in white marble. Mispronounced "Pig Alley," the area became what one American journalist called "the tenderloin of Paris," the first stop for anyone in search of bad girls and a good time. Of the sculptor who bore its name, one writer commented, "He would certainly have been extremely unhappy had he known what a suggestive, sultry sound his name now has for millions of people."

At 10 p.m., as other Parisians put on their pajamas and brushed their teeth, postwar Montmartre came to life. "A good hundred thousand people have just woken up," explained one writer. "They depend for their living on the nights of Paris. Waiters, dancers, singers, night-club doorkeepers, musicians, throwers-out, photographers, cloakroom attendants, conjurers, police inspectors in plain clothes, dishwashers, mannequins, in fact the entire flora and fauna of more or less serious ladies and gentleman who in one way or another live on their charms or on each other."

Joseph Wechsberg, a musician in Paris before the war returning in 1945 as a GI, found Montmartre little changed. "The women accordionists in the cafés were still playing their old songs and javas, the tired sidewalk painters had their watercolours propped up against the trees of the Boulevard de Clichy, and the busy, smiling little ladies [i.e., prostitutes] were patrolling up and down as of old, almost as chic as ever despite three-year-old dresses and wooden shoes." (With leather unobtainable, shoemakers adapted the traditional peasant footwear, clogs whittled from pine.)

Despite the presence everywhere of free-spending American servicemen, Montmartre's barmen, waiters, and musicians lamented the departure of the even more spendthrift Germans. In scenes reminiscent of the film *Casablanca,* they would order expensive champagne, get drunk, become maudlin, and demand that the band play German music, only to lose their temper when the musicians subversively wove a few bars of "La Marseillaise" into "Deutschland über Alles."

Seeing how effectively the Montmartrois sold pleasure, style, and sensual gratification, France in general did the same, but on a grander scale. As Édith Piaf's own composition "La Vie en Rose" became an overnight classic, she toured the United States and South America, backed by a small male choir, Les Compagnons de la Chanson, the leader of which, inevitably, she took as her lover. The distribution overseas of films made under the occupation, such as *Les Visiteurs du Soir* (*The Night Visitors*) and *Les Enfants du Paradis* (*Children of Paradise*), reminded international audiences of France's prewar eminence in cinema. Vignerons publicized French wine and restaurateurs the joys of haute cuisine, their enthusiasm echoed by such expatriates as Julia Child. Moving to Paris with her husband in 1948, Child credited her first experience of French cooking with "an opening up of the soul and spirit."

Of the elements that distinguished prewar France, only fashion lagged. Nobody was surprised. In a climate of austerity, who would wish to wear expensive clothing, or have the money to buy it? Nobody anticipated that haute couture would play a key role in restoring France to the center of the world stage, thanks to the imagination of one man, an obscure designer named Christian Dior.

THE NEW LOOK

During the war, most Parisian fashion houses shut down for lack of materials and staff. No sooner had peace returned than unions demanded higher wages for the seamstresses who sewed each gown by hand. Despite the undoubted justice of their claim, the campaign backfired on them, since French couturiers, already under pressure from foreign manufacturers, cut back on haute couture in favor of prêt-à-porter: ready-to-wear clothing, factory-cut in the most popular sizes. Within a decade, marketing through department stores would render bespoke dress-making, except for the extremely wealthy, a thing of the past.

Awaiting the first postwar designs from French fashion houses, the editors of *Vogue* and *Harper's Bazaar* expected warmed-over wartime styles; plain clothing, conservatively made from cheap materials. Nothing prepared them for the collection unveiled in February 1947 by Christian Dior, a little-known designer long associated with the conservative house of Lucien Lelong.

Of wartime austerity, there was no sign. Instead, his ensembles exploded with a baroque extravagance not seen on Parisian catwalks since the twenties. Under vast hats, costumes with nipped-in waists and tight buttoned jackets flared into multiple petticoats and skirts that brushed the ground. Dior called the collection *Corolle*, the botanical term for a circle of flower petals, but Carmel Snow of *Harper's Bazaar* coined the phrase that stuck, calling it simply "The New Look."

Eric Newby, then running a London fashion house, applauded Dior's creations.

> They marked the re-birth of women as they had always existed in the minds of men—provocative, ostensibly helpless and made for love. He immobilised them in exquisite dresses which contained between fifteen and twenty-five yards of material; dresses with tiny sashed waists in black broadcloth, tussore and silk taffeta, each with a built-in corset which was itself a deeply disturbing work of art. By day, superb beneath huge hats that resembled elegant mushrooms, they were unable to run; by night they needed help when entering a taxi. As these divine visions moved, their underskirts gave out a rustling sound that was indescribably sweet to the ear.

While buyers for American stores struggled to adapt Dior's innovations to the mass market, wealthy clients besieged his atelier to be fitted for the real thing, no matter what the cost. First in line were Paris's expensive call girls. Whether dining in chic restaurants or loitering in the lobbies of four-star hotels, they were living advertisements for his work.

Not everyone admired Dior's inventiveness. To ordinary French women, the New Look represented conspicuous consumption at its most flagrant. "It took a lot of nerve," wrote a Dior biographer, "to flaunt such opulence in a country paralyzed by strikes, rocked by government crises, and seemingly doomed to perpetual gloom." Resentment sometimes deteriorated into abuse, even violence. Author Nancy Mitford, who bought a suit from the collection, complained that "people shout *ordures* at you from vans, because for some reason it creates class feeling in a way no sables would." *Paris Match* photographer Walter Carone, looking for fresh backgrounds, took his mannequins to a street market on Montmartre's rue Lepic, but as soon as they stepped out into the street in their New Look dresses, local women attacked them, yanking their hair and ripping the gowns.

Critics of Dior suggested his lavish use of expensive fabrics had something to do with textile manufacturer Marcel Boussac, who invested 60 million francs in his company. Scornfully, Dior pointed out that Boussac's factories produced only cotton, a fabric entirely too everyday for his exotic creations. Coco Chanel, more familiar than most with the dark side of the fashion business, saw no calculation in the New Look. Rather, it signified the revival of France's national pride and the couture that had always been as integral a part of that culture as its cuisine and wine. "Fashion is not something that exists in dresses only," she said. "Fashion is in the sky, in the street; fashion has to do with ideas, the way we live, what is happening."

Christian Dior's New Look. "The re-birth of women as they had always existed in the minds of men."

❋ · 19 · ❋

BOOKS ON THE BUTTE

Unlike painters, France's writers traditionally avoided the limelight. Literature to them was less a job than a calling, on a par with the law or the church. They scorned the self-advertisement of American expatriates and their practice of writing in cafés. A French author would no more pursue his profession in public than would a dentist.

A number of writers, most of them French, preferred Montmartre for its anonymity and privacy. Most made their homes in a cluster of streets along the northern margin of the butte. For a while, Raymond Queneau, author of the playfully Surrealist novel *Zazie dans le Métro*, lived in a hotel on rue Caulaincourt. A neighbor was Francis Carco, whose books about Montmartre's colorful history earned him the title *"romancier des apaches"*—the gangsters' novelist. Louis-Ferdinand Céline, author of *Voyage au Bout de la Nuit* (*Journey to the End of the Night*), practiced as an obstetrician on rue Girardon. At the same time, his virulently anti-Semitic pamphlets led to a postwar conviction for collaboration.

Few of Montmartre's obscure corners were more secluded than Cité Veron, an impasse running down the side of the Moulin Rouge. Once the haunt of petty thieves, it developed into a community of rehearsal studios, public baths, workshops, and a few rooftop apartments. In 1953, poet and screenwriter Jacques Prévert rented one of these. It remained his home for thirty years. His neighbor was Boris Vian, jazz-loving novelist and central figure in postwar Saint-Germain. After playing trumpet all night in the smoke-filled cellar of Le Tabou, Vian would slip away to the peace of his meticulously maintained apartment, which included, paradoxically, a workshop devoted to his second profession, that of engineer.

Of the few expatriates who settled in Montmartre, the best-known was Henry Miller. Between 1932 and 1934, he and Alfred Perlès shared an apartment on Clichy's Avenue Anatole France, its windows looking out on a dispiriting industrial landscape of factory roofs and railway yards. A bastion of communism inhabited mainly by factory workers, Clichy was, for Miller, a better representation of Paris than trendy Montparnasse. A connoisseur of Paris's secret places, he relished his intimacy with a district about which tourists knew nothing, and celebrated the period and the place in the 1956 book *Quiet Days in Clichy*, illustrated with photographs by the Hungarian Gyula Halász, known as Brassaï.

Miller's particular haunt was the Wepler, a brasserie on Place Clichy, the hangout of petty criminals, pimps, and prostitutes. "The rosy glow which suffused the place," he wrote, "emanated from the cluster of whores who usually congregated near the entrance. As they gradually distributed themselves among the clientele, the place became not only warm and rosy but fragrant. They fluttered about in the dimming light like perfumed fireflies."

The literary personality most associated in the public mind with Montmartre never existed. Mimi Pinson, a poor seamstress with a heart of gold, appears in Alfred de Musset's 1845 *Mimi Pinson: Profile of a Grisette*. Living in a tiny attic room on rue Mont Cenis, her only companion a pet finch ("Pinson" means finch), Mimi is loved by everyone. After she pawns her only good dress for money to feed a friend, other friends redeem the pledge and hurry to her house to return the dress, only to find she has gone to mass at Saint-Sulpice church. But what did she wear? Musset explains:

> She had on, in lieu of a gown, a petticoat of dark calico, half hidden by a green serge curtain, of

which she had contrived to make herself a sort of shawl. She had wrapped herself in her curtain with so much art and care that it really looked like an old shawl, and the border could hardly be seen. In short, she contrived to be charming even in this toggery, and to prove, for the thousandth time, that a pretty woman is always pretty.

"Mimi Pinson" came to signify the kindhearted working girl, a symbol of "making do," "helping out," "carrying on." Puccini acknowledged her as the basis of Mimi of *La Bohème*. Utrillo painted the house where she is supposed to have lived. The statue *La Grisette de 1830* by Jean-Bernard Descomps that stands on Place Jules Ferry in the eleventh arrondissement is believed to represent her. The trade union formed by seamstresses called itself the Mimi Pinson Association. In 1902, composer Gustave Charpentier opened the Conservatoire Populaire Mimi Pinson, which for more than thirty-five years offered free musical training to seamstresses. Musset's story even reached as far as Atlanta, since Margaret Mitchell in *Gone with the Wind* had Scarlett O'Hara adapt her mother's green velvet curtains into a gown.

THE MAN WHO WALKED
THROUGH WALLS

Among the oddest literary monuments in Paris is a statue on Place Marcel Aymé, a tiny square off Montmartre's rue Norvins. The life-size bronze figure shows a man emerging from a stone wall after having, it seems, walked through it. Half of his body is free, but anyone who knows the story that inspired it, Marcel Aymé's "Le Passe-Muraille" or "The Walker Through Walls," will know that its subject, an otherwise placid civil servant named Dutilleul, is doomed to remain there indefinitely.

Initially, Dutilleul sees no practical application for his superpower—not until, that is, he loses his temper with his boss and decides to give him a scare.

> He rose from his chair and entered the wall which separated his office from that of the associate director. He was careful to move only partway through the wall, so that just his head emerged on the other side.
>
> Monsieur Lécuyer was seated at his work table, his ever-twitching pen shifting a comma

in the text an employee had submitted to him for approval. Hearing a quiet cough in his office, he looked up, and discovered to his unspeakable alarm the head (just the head) of Dutilleul stuck to the wall like a hunting trophy. What's more, the head was alive. It looked over its pince-nez glasses at him with deepest hatred. And then it began to speak.

"Monsieur," it said, "you are a hoodlum, a boor, and a spoiled brat."

Having induced his boss's mental breakdown, Dutilleul develops a taste for bad behavior. He can walk into the bedroom of his married mistress without her husband being any the wiser, burgle the best-protected homes, even stroll out of the jail where he's imprisoned. All is going well until he injudiciously experiments with cures for his condition, and is left permanently locked in a stone wall. Periodically, someone who knows his secret takes an accordion down to where Dutilleul is imprisoned and plays a few tunes to relieve the monotony of his life.

Actor Jean Marais, who dabbled in sculpture after his retirement, created the statue in 1989 to honor the writer, who lived nearby. The face is a portrait of Aymé, and the touches of visitors have worn the patina from his left hand. Do they hope to end Dutilleul's imprisonment by drawing him out of the wall? Sadly, unlike the sword Excalibur, he is locked forever in the stone.

Jean Marais's statue of Marcel Aymé.

THE BISTRO DU CURÉ

Arriving in Paris in the winter of 1989, I made it my business to explore Montmartre. Following the obligatory visits to Sacré-Coeur and the Lapin Agile, I dutifully attended a movie at the tiny Studio 28 on steeply sloping rue Tholozé, paying my respects to the cinema where, in 1930, right-wing mobs broke up a screening of the Dalí/Buñuel *L'Age d'Or* and believing, wrongly, that the film was foreign and Communist, wrecked an exhibition of Surrealist art in the foyer.

Except for evocations of the belle époque, generally mocked up in studios far from the real thing, modern filmmakers show little interest in Montmartre. The most recent success, the quirky 2001 comedy adventure *Le Fabuleux Destin de Amélie Poulain* made a star of Audrey Tautou and turned the otherwise unremarkable Café des 2 Moulins at 15 rue Lepic into a tourist destination, but that film ranges far wider than the hillsides of Montmartre.

If any film captures a sense of Montmartre at its most vivid, it's the 1955 *French Cancan*, written and directed by Jean Renoir, son of Pierre-Auguste, and starring Jean Gabin as Henri Danglard, the failed entrepreneur who retrieves his fortune by reviving the traditional dance and teaching a group of laundry girls how to perform it. Françoise Arnoul is his star dancer Nini Pattes-en-l'Air, and Maria Félix demonstrates the belly dance à la Madame Zaléska.

Danglard believes, correctly, that polite society will flock to Montmartre to sample the most outrageous behavior, providing there's no accompanying risk. "A taste of the low life for millionaires," he promises. "Adventure in comfort. Garden tables, the best champagne, great numbers by the finest artistes. The bourgeois will be thrilled to mix with our girls without fear of disease or getting knifed."

After those first visits, I usually avoided Montmartre. Who wanted to browse the scores of sex shops along Boulevard de Clichy, trudge through display cases of phallic idols in the Museum of Eroticism, or dodge the three-card-trick artists on rue de Steinkerque, let alone endure the professional froufrou of the Moulin Rouge?

Then a friend invited me to lunch at 21 Boulevard de Clichy. Tucked between two emporia, their windows liberally stocked with whips, manacles, and improbable underwear, a discreet sign identified our destination as the Bistro du Curé—the Priest's Café.

"I think you'll like this," said my friend with a leer.

Steeling myself for topless waitresses dipping more than their thumbs in the soup, I was surprised to be served by middle-aged ladies with all the allure of the nuns who taught me in grade school.

Nuns . . . yes, that's where I'd seen that gravitas before, the righteous look of *This hurts me more than it hurts you.* One felt that not to order the day's special would bring a stinging whack on the ear, while to ask for beer or wine—neither on the menu—would have been a mortal sin.

Then there were the discreet crosses on the wall, and a small anonymous door at the back of the room from which the occasional person emerged. Though obviously connected with the sex trade in some way or other, all appeared subdued, even contrite.

"It's a chapel?" I suggested.

My friend's face fell. "Yes," he said, annoyed at how quickly I'd caught on. "The waitresses are all nuns." He nodded toward the door. "And there's a church upstairs."

After our coffee, he led me up a narrow flight of stairs to a tiny chapel on the minuscule altar of which burned a red lamp, signifying that the Holy Sacrament was present. From behind heavy curtains, the mumble of a confession was faintly audible. Making as little noise as possible on the bare wood floor, we slipped away.

Intrigued, I read up on this curious establishment. A mission to the sinners of Montmartre disguised as a café, it came under the management of the nearby Église de la Sainte-Trinité, but my friend was wrong about the staff being nuns. For fourteen years, a rotating team of 180 parishioners did the serving, cooking, and cleaning up, while a priest was present for part of every day "to serve tourists, prostitutes, transsexuals, and other inhabitants of the quartier."

The Bistro du Curé closed in 2002, not because there were too few sinners along the boulevard but because they were too numerous. To convert this village of sin, nothing less than a cathedral would suffice. But its longevity said something about this most paradoxical of Paris's arrondissements. A district that produced a headless but still talking saint, a theater of horrors, phantom cabarets, an uprising that might have transformed the world, and a community of artists who, in their way, did just that, would view a consecrated café with, at most, a lifted eyebrow and a shrug. *Ça, c'est Montmartre.*

AFTERWORD

LOVE, IT'S SO SIMPLE

IF I SEEM TO HOLD A BRIEF FOR MONTMARTRE AS THE DIS-
trict where radical changes are a matter of course, you can
put it down to personal experience. Were it not for Montmartre and an incident that took place there, I would not
now be living in Paris.

All Paris stories are to some extent stories of love—
love requited or unrequited, knowing or innocent, spiritual, intellectual, perverted, doomed. The love that brought
me to Paris combined a little of them all, as a poorly written
movie tries to cram in everything that might draw an audience. My story featured coincidence, the supernatural (or
something very like it), Hollywood, and a long-lost love
miraculously rekindled. . . . Cheap romantic nonsense, I
would have said had I seen it onscreen.

Living in Los Angeles in 1989, on the rebound from a

broken marriage, I'd become friendly with Suzy, a woman in mid-level movie management whose longtime lover, an irascible and addictive filmmaker, had recently died. Though he'd treated her with casual cruelty, she felt bereft without him, particularly since she'd lost most of her relatives to Hitler.

"If only I could be sure that we would be reunited someday," she said tearfully, "I think I could go on."

As a practical woman in the movie business, Suzy put this concept into preproduction. With me as company, she began to audition systems of belief, looking for one that would guarantee reunion with her lover after death. We visited card readers and mediums, and a spiritist church in Encino, where the audience sat enthralled as an elderly lady, seated at a card table with her devoted husband holding her hand, gabbled in what we were told was the voice of the famous medium Edgar Cayce. At one point, the phrase "anti-Christ" surfaced from the babble. An instant later, a tiny earth tremor shook the hall. We exchanged significant glances with our neighbors. Aaah!

"Fuck this," Suzy murmured. "I feel like eating Mexican. How about you?"

The last candidate was a man in the remote suburb of City of Commerce, who needed subjects who would agree to be hypnotized as part of some ill-defined project. Suzy didn't feel like surrendering control of her mind unless somebody she trusted had done so before, so she dispatched me into that wilderness of twenty-four-hour poker clubs and used-car lots to check him out.

Joe was a young psychologist who believed that we've all lived before in other bodies. As part of his work at a mental hospital, he used hypnosis a lot, and was convinced that, in a trance, people might reveal that, in another life, they had met Jesus Christ. I told him frankly that the works of the Blessed Shirley MacLaine had inoculated me against this concept. Any lingering belief was extinguished by the regiments of cocktail waitresses and bus drivers claiming to be the reincarnations of Napoleon, Cleopatra, and the Queen of Sheba.

"Well, OK," Joe said amiably. "But as long as you're here, why not give it a try?"

That session and those that followed in Joe's poky little apartment were revelatory. He never pushed me back into any former existence, but along the way I did re-experience some startling events in my own life that I'd presumably suppressed. After half a dozen visits, however, it became clear that any former lives I might have had were so boring that I'd slept through them.

With a sigh, Joe finally accepted defeat. "But I really appreciate your time, John. And I'd like to give you a gift."

As I looked around his threadbare apartment, trying to think of a diplomatic way to refuse, he went on, "I don't mean money. I mean a post-hypnotic gift. Think of the three things that have given you greatest pleasure in life. Then, as you name each, I'll squeeze your left wrist. And from now on, every time you squeeze that wrist you'll re-experience the same pleasure."

My choices, nominated while still in a trance, astonished me. Not great sex, wild music, drug highs, or roller-coaster rides—just the solitary pleasures of someone who, though usually surrounded by people, felt himself alone.

The first was the pleasure of getting up before the sun, and sitting down in the predawn silence with a cup of coffee to start writing.

The second was the memory of a song, "Finishing the Hat," from Stephen Sondheim's *Sunday in the Park with George*, about the painter Georges Seurat. While he paints the great canvas *A Sunday Afternoon on the Island of La Grande Jatte*, agonizing about how to render in tiny points of color the reality of something as prosaic as a hat, his exasperated mistress is lured away by a man who, though no Seurat, can give her the love and attention she needs.

The song he sings when he finds her gone can still bring tears to my eyes. It did when I saw the show in New

York, and I wept again lying on Joe's worn corduroy couch. The tears were still wet on my face when he asked for my third choice. Again, it astonished me. And again, it was connected with Paris.

Years before, I'd been romantically involved with a young Frenchwoman named Marie-Dominique. We'd traveled around the world together and had wonderful times, but her life as a radio journalist in Paris and mine as a writer in America or Australia drew us apart.

Now, in a memory so vivid that I felt I'd been physically transported back ten years and across the world, I was standing with her on a winter's day in the huge flea market of Clignancourt, on the outskirts of Montmartre. We were eating thin French fries with mustard out of a cone of paper. I could taste the salt and the fat, see the wind ruffling the fur collar of her coat, feel the cold through my feet. Emotions too complex to analyze lifted me like a wave.

Driving back home in a daze, I rang Marie-Dominique in Paris. Wouldn't she like to visit me in Los Angeles? Not long after, she did.

From the moment she got off the plane, we both sensed a fundamental change in our relationship. Ten years before, I'd been married and she'd been starting her career. Now my marriage was over, and she, still unmarried, was established as one of France's top radio journalists. Like a bottle of wine that only comes into its best after it's had time to breathe, our love was ready to drink.

For the next ten days, we barely spent a minute apart. And in the quiet times, almost without discussing it, we became aware that this part of our lives was coming to a close. We would return to Paris, set up a home, marry, have children.

Within three weeks, to the astonishment of my friends, I'd emptied my apartment, disposed of my possessions, and booked a flight to Paris, a city where I'd never lived, in a country where I knew nobody, and whose language

Wedding in 1991; myself, Marie-Dominique, and baby Louise.

I couldn't speak. I was fifty, Marie-Dominique ten years younger, and nobody believed it would last a fortnight, if indeed it survived as far as the airport.

They could not have been more wrong. But then, they hadn't reckoned on one thing.

They hadn't reckoned on Montmartre.

ACKNOWLEDGMENTS

MY GRATITUDE, AS ALWAYS, TO MY EDITOR PETER HUB-bard and the creative team at Harper Perennial. Also to my agent, Jonathan Lloyd at Curtis Brown London, and to Tony Foster for his sterling design expertise. *Afterword: Love, It's So Simple* . . . first appeared in a different form in *We'll Always Have Paris: Sex and Love in the City of Light* (HarperPerennial, 2005).

CREDITS

The author has made every reasonable effort to trace the ownership of copyrighted material included in this book and to make full acknowledgment of its use.

INDEX

Photo by Rudy Gelenter

ABOUT THE AUTHOR

JOHN BAXTER has lived in Paris for more than twenty years. He is the author of many critically acclaimed books about France, including *Saint-Germain-des-Prés: Paris's Rebel Quarter, Five Nights in Paris: After Dark in the City of Light, The Perfect Meal: In Search of the Lost Tastes of France* (winner of the IACP Cookbook Award for Culinary Travel), *The Most Beautiful Walk in the World: A Pedestrian in Paris, Immoveable Feast: A Paris Christmas, Paris at the End of the World,* and *We'll Always Have Paris: Sex and Love in the City of Light.* Baxter, who gives iterary walking tours through Paris, is also a film critic and biographer whose subjects have included the directors Federico Fellini, Stanley Kubrick, Woody Allen, and, most recently, Josef von Sternberg. Born in Australia, Baxter lives with his wife and daughter in the Saint-Germain-des-Prés neighborhood, in the building Sylvia Beach once called home.

www.johnbaxterparis.com

BOOKS BY JOHN BAXTER

Great Parisian Neighborhoods
SAINT-GERMAIN-DES-PRÉS
Paris's Rebel Quarter
Available in Paperback and E-Book

A unique blend of history, memoir, and sightseeing essentials, as the award-winning chronicler of life in Paris reveals the secrets of his home quarter.

THE MOST BEAUTIFUL WALK IN THE WORLD
A Pedestrian in Paris
Available in Paperback and E-Book

NATIONAL BESTSELLER

Baxter reveals the most beautiful walks through Paris, including the favorite routes of artists and writers who have called the city home.

FIVE NIGHTS IN PARIS
After Dark in the City of Light
Available in Paperback and E-Book

John Baxter introduces you to the city's streets after dark, revealing hidden treasures and unexpected delights as he takes you through five of the city's greatest neighborhoods.

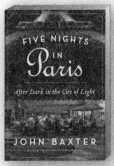

WE'LL ALWAYS HAVE PARIS
Sex and Love in the City of Light
Available in Paperback and E-Book

"A charming insider's guide to literary and artistic Paris. . . . Excellent." —*Daily Mail* (London)

THE PERFECT MEAL

Available in Paperback and E-Book
IACP COOKBOOK AWARD WINNER (*Culinary Travel*)

"Full of humor, insight, and mouth-watering details, *The Perfect Meal* is a delightful tour of 'traditional' French culture and cuisine." —*Travel + Leisure*

IMMOVEABLE FEAST
A Paris Christmas

Available in Paperback and E-Book

The charming, funny, and improbable tale of how a man who was raised on white bread—and didn't speak a word of French—ended up preparing the annual Christmas dinner for a venerable Parisian family.

PARIS AT THE END OF THE WORLD
The City of Light During the Great War, 1914-1918

Available in Paperback and E-Book

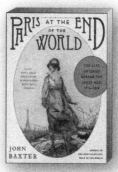

John Baxter brings to life one of the most dramatic and fascinating periods in Paris's history. As World War I ravaged France, the City of Light blazed more brightly than ever. Despite the terrifying sounds that could be heard from the capital, Parisians lived with urgency and without inhibition. The rich hosted wild parties, artists such as Picasso reached new heights, and the war brought a wave of foreigners, including Ernest Hemingway, to Paris for the first time. In this brilliant book, Baxter shows how the Great War forged the spirit of the city we love today.